Praise for

"*Healing into Possibility* re͟ surrender and a time to b mined to engage in the tr sis. I needed to stop reading Alison's text periodically and just think. This is the mark of an important book — inner looking."

— Jeanne Achterberg, professor, Saybrook Graduate School
and Research Institute and author of *Imagery in Healing*,
*Rituals of Healing*, and *Woman as Healer*

"I have repeatedly seen Alison Bonds Shapiro positively affect the attitudes of patients at crucial points in their recoveries. What Alison teaches can be helpful to everyone, regardless of their circumstances."

— Michelle Camicia, MSN, CRRN, director, Rehabilitation
Operations, Kaiser Foundation Rehabilitation Center

"Alison Shapiro unexpectedly met herself along the roadway of her life and, practicing courage, discipline, and mindfulness, learned that healing begins within. From the trauma of brain stem strokes, she discovered her greatest resource: the psyche's desire to heal, to grow, and through us to bring something more fully into the world. While forever changed and deepened, her dialogue with the psyche led her back to an engaged, productive life."

— James Hollis, PhD, Jungian analyst and author of
*What Matters Most: Living a More Considered Life*

"*Healing into Possibility* skillfully illuminates the path from tragedy to transformation. While Alison's strokes may have caused a degree of brain damage, her mind has become as clear as her heart is open. This is an uplifting book full of good common sense. It beautifully illustrates that healing is much more than a response to good medical care. It's a spiritual practice."

— Frank Ostaseski, founder,
Metta Institute and Zen Hospice Project

"This book is a night-light for times of darkness and loss, enabling us each to find our own way home to our wholeness and the rest of our lives. *Healing into Possibility* will remind you of the hidden power in every human being, including yourself."
— Rachel Naomi Remen, MD, author of
*Kitchen Table Wisdom* and *My Grandfather's Blessings*

"Alison Bonds Shapiro's authentic and optimistic account of her recovery from a series of brain hemorrhages gives not only hope but a pragmatic approach that will be helpful to those who experience this kind of life-changing event. By telling her story, with insights at every turn, she has provided not just a 'good read' but a very important book for patients, families, and healthcare providers who live in the world she has experienced."
— M. Elizabeth Sandel, MD, chief, Physical Medicine and
Rehabilitation, Kaiser Foundation Rehabilitation Center

"*Healing into Possibility* comes from the author's heart and will give readers what its title states. It can coach you and help to transform you so you can live up to your potential."
— Dr. Bernie S. Siegel, author of *365 Prescriptions for the Soul*

"This extraordinary story of recovery bears witness to the power of intention and perseverance in healing and transformation. In this inspiring account of her personal journey, the author brings hope to anyone struggling to overcome physical limitations and aspiring to engage in a fulfilling and meaningful life."
— Frances Vaughan, PhD, psychologist and author of
*Shadows of the Sacred*

# HEALING
## —— INTO ——
# POSSIBILITY

# HEALING
## — INTO —
# POSSIBILITY

*the transformational lessons
of a stroke*

## Alison Bonds Shapiro
### Foreword by James S. Gordon, MD

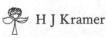 H J Kramer

*published in a joint venture with*

 New World Library
Novato, California

An H J Kramer book
*published in a joint venture with*
New World Library

| | |
|---|---|
| Editorial office: | Administrative office: |
| H J Kramer Inc. | New World Library |
| P.O. Box 1082 | 14 Pamaron Way |
| Tiburon, California 94920 | Novato, California 94949 |

The material in this book is intended for education. It is not meant to take the place of diagnosis and treatment by a qualified medical practitioner or therapist. No expressed or implied guarantee as to the effects of the use of the recommendations can be given nor liability taken. The author's experiences throughout this book are true, although some identifying details such as name and location have been changed to protect the privacy of others.

Edited by Nancy Carleton
Text design and typography by Tona Pearce Myers

Library of Congress Cataloging-in-Publication Data
Shapiro, Alison Bonds.
Healing into possibility : the transformational lessons of a stroke / Alison Bonds Shapiro ; foreword by James S. Gordon.
    p.   cm.
ISBN 978-1-932073-24-9 (pbk. : alk. paper)
    1. Shapiro, Alison Bonds—Health. 2. Cerebrovascular disease—Patients—Biography. 3. Cerebrovascular disease—Patients—Rehabilitation. I. Title.
RC388.5.S467 2009
362.196'810092—dc22
[B]                                                                          2009008487

First printing, June 2009
ISBN 978-1-932073-24-9
Printed in Canada on 100% postconsumer-waste recycled paper

New World Library is a proud member of the Green Press Initiative.

10  9  8  7  6  5  4  3  2  1

*To my grandchildren, Patrick, Alaric, Liam, and Jonah,
who dwell in possibility*

*Every great loss demands that we choose life again.*
— RACHEL NAOMI REMEN, *My Grandfather's Blessings*

# Contents

# Foreword

Healing into Possibility is Alison Bonds Shapiro's account of her remarkable recovery from two life-threatening, life-challenging bleeds into her brain stem, the part of the nervous system that governs our most vital functions, including breathing and heartbeat. It is an enormously inspiring and deeply practical guide for anyone who has been affected by a stroke, an accident, or any other form of cataclysmic injury.

Alison takes us step-by-step — actually, hand-in-hand is the way it felt to me — on her journey. She begins with her initial disbelief and denial — just a little "low blood sugar" she thought, as she began to wobble on her feet — and continues through the fear and despair she experienced as she came to realize the threat to her life and the damage to her way of living that the two strokes brought with them. Waking in a hospital bed, she discovered that she could no longer control her bowels or bladder, that she could not speak or see clearly or move her left arm or leg. Later she found out that she, like others who suffer brain stem strokes, had had a less than 50 percent chance of survival.

We move ahead slowly, often painfully, with Alison. She makes us feel the grueling pull and tug of mental and physical effort as she works with wonderful, tough, and gifted physical therapists to regain the use of her limbs, one small muscle group at a time. She shares with us relevant and highly encouraging information on neuroplasticity, the brain's ability to retool itself in the aftermath of great damage. And she shows us, in the kitchen and bedroom and on the trails outside her mountain home, how she learns to "live around" her limitations, reclaiming, over arduous months, her ability to read and walk, cook and paint and climb.

Alison's writing — spare, matter of fact, even stripped down — is intimate and believable. She shows rather than tells us that we are witnessing a miracle of recovery that may well be accessible to any of us who is similarly affected, and we are moved and believe her.

All this would be more than enough for any book, but it is only one part, one grace of *Healing into Possibility*. "I was beginning," Alison tells us near the beginning of her journey, "to learn that it's not what happens to us that matters" but "how we deal with what happens to us." And throughout the story of her physical recovery, Alison shares with us, without fanfare or self-importance, lessons that we can apply in lives as yet untouched by physical calamity. There are many of them, and because she is so candid about her own struggles, so unaffected in offering them to us, they are easy for us to read, believe, assimilate, and perhaps even live by.

Alison begins by urging us to accept what comes to us without laboring to uncover an explanation or discover a cause, without endlessly asking "Why me?" This question, she tells us with characteristic directness, "simply doesn't go anywhere." It "perpetuate[s] the fantasy that life is fair." Far more important is looking at what is possible — here is where she invokes the exhilarating hopefulness of recent discoveries about neuroplasticity — and beginning the work of living up to that possibility. "Problems" she reminds us, so simply, so helpfully, "are solved by looking for solutions." And, she adds, wisely, by finding, along with dedicated therapeutic problem solvers, "a reason to live." Hers: "I owed it [to my sons] to set an example that when life is hard, we find a way to deal with it."

Each step in Alison's recovery, in the journey that is her new life, is marked by a hard-won, luminous discovery for her readers as well as herself: about the educational and inspirational value of others' solutions — ones in Alison's case devised by friends with strokes and other neurological disabilities; about the humbling, enriching need for an independent person like her to learn to rely on others; about the great learning, and relaxation, that can come from "welcom[ing] everything" and "push[ing] away nothing"; about the colossal importance of taking and valuing the smallest of steps in recovery; about the paradoxical understanding that in caring for oneself, we are — because of our connection to others, our interdependency — also caring for them; and, most touchingly to me, about the realization that she could be — indeed, was — loved not for what she did in the world or for others but just for herself. "I'd never," she tells us, "truly seen the place in other people's hearts I occupied."

I was very happy to read *Healing into Possibility*. Alison Bonds Shapiro has a wonderful knack, befitting a dedicated cook, of seasoning old and even difficult lessons with the warmth and variety of her own experience; of making hardships that had seemed barely palatable delicious, nourishing, and easily assimilated. "My strokes happened," she tells us toward the end of the book, "I healed, and now it is my privilege to live out the lessons I learned from them." It is our privilege, and our delight, to learn the deep psychological and spiritual — and human — lessons she is teaching, and, perhaps, to learn with her to live them out in our own lives.

— James S. Gordon, MD, author of
*Unstuck: Your Guide to the Seven-Stage Journey Out of Depression* and founder and director of
The Center for Mind-Body Medicine in Washington, DC

# A Story of Transformation

I SURVIVED TWO STROKES. There's nothing all that remark-able about this fact. Around 700,000 new strokes occur in the United States every year, one every forty-five seconds, according to the American Heart Association. Most likely you know someone, or know of someone, who has had a stroke. Maybe you've had one yourself.

But this isn't a story about someone who survived a stroke. This is a story of transformation. My strokes became the stage on which I experienced the lessons of transformation I was to learn. What's remarkable about this story is what my strokes taught me. I couldn't have predicted how much I would learn and keep on learning from what happened. I continue to be surprised and amazed and infinitely grateful for what I'm now able to do with that knowledge. That's the reason I'm writing this book — to share my amazement and my gratitude. I'm not writing to tell you about my misery. Everybody has his or her own misery. You don't need mine.

For the last three years I've been teaching these lessons of transformation. The opportunity to put these lessons into service to help others is, in itself, deeply transformative. By sharing the stories of our lives, the truth of our experiences, we give one another a profound gift, rich with meaning. I've had the great privilege of hearing the stories of many people when I give talks. Their stories never fail to touch and inspire me. I've included some of them in this book, where I hope they'll inspire you too.

When I teach at a rehabilitation center, my classes typically include stroke survivors; people with brain injuries, neurological diseases, spinal cord injuries, or other problems; and family members, friends, and medical staff. Almost universally, people who attend tell me that the lessons I share help with whatever life challenges they're facing, not just with physical recovery.

I've applied the lessons I share in this book to the rest of my life. I've taught them in a variety of contexts, both business and personal. Again and again, I get the feedback that these lessons help people find a way to transform their own lives. The other day a woman said to me, "You've completely changed my attitude. Now I believe I can make a difference in my own life." There can be no greater reward for sharing what I know than that.

Over and over again, I've witnessed this simple truth: We can change the outcome of what happens to us. We have the power, through the way we approach our challenges, to make a difference in every aspect of our lives. I've lived this myself, and I've watched other people live this. The tools are accessible to anyone. Giving talks, writing this book, and telling my story and the stories of others are my ways of sharing the tools. When we're connected by one another's stories, our potential for transformation is boundless.

One of my greatest joys these days is knowing that these tools and stories help other people. I hope that what I've written is a benefit to you. I hope that reading this book enables you to see more clearly that you are the person who has the power to have the most profound impact on your own life.

Blessings,
Alison Bonds Shapiro
Winter 2009

# PART ONE
# SHOWING UP

# CHAPTER ONE

## *Strokes Happen*

IN MAY OF 2002 I had two brain-stem hemorrhages twenty-four hours apart — two strokes — which left me profoundly disabled. Today I'm no longer profoundly disabled. Today I'm more empowered than I've ever been. Who could have imagined the way this would unfold? I certainly couldn't, not in the early days, when I thought that maybe surviving a brain-stem stroke wasn't such a great idea — that maybe I'd be better off dead than disabled. At the time, I had a 50/50 chance of surviving. Only 50 percent of people who have brain-stem hemorrhages live. I could just as easily have died. And for a while I was sorry I hadn't.

So what was the setting for my transformation? Who was I when I had the strokes? The basic facts are these: I was fifty-five years old. I was reasonably fit. I exercised regularly. I didn't smoke, and I didn't drink. I had low blood pressure. I was free of diabetes, and ate a good diet. I had no risk factors for a stroke that anybody could have discerned. I was happy. I loved my husband. I loved my life. I lived in a beautiful place. My children were grown and out of the house. I was in the middle of fulfilling a lifelong dream. None of this seemed to matter much. I had a stroke anyway.

These days I pay attention to stroke literature. No big surprise. We all tend to pay attention to the things that are up close and personal. Most stroke literature talks about preventing strokes. Prevention is good and important work. Many conditions exacerbate the risk of stroke and can and should be controlled. Nobody who thinks about it wants to encourage anyone to have a stroke. But the point is that strokes happen regardless, and there's so much more we can learn about what to do after a stroke. And we can learn what this experience — and what any powerful, life-changing experience — has to teach us.

On May 3, 2002, I woke up and got out of bed to go to the bathroom. It was morning, around seven o'clock, on a lovely warm day. I'd gone to bed early the night before and was well rested, eager to get back to work on my lifelong dream. When I stood up, I noticed that I felt shaky. I walked the very short distance to the bathroom, noticing the slightly odd way I was walking. I sat down on the toilet to pee; I knew I was urinating because I could hear myself, but I couldn't feel it. "How strange," I thought.

I have a tendency to experience low blood sugar, so my next thought was "This is the worst case of low blood sugar I've ever had." I headed to the kitchen to get a piece of fruit as a quick way to raise my sugar level. Our house is small. The kitchen shares a wall with the bathroom and the bedroom, and its far side opens into the living room. I came out the bathroom door, turned left, and reached for a piece of fruit. The nearest was an orange, which required that I either peel it or cut it. Cutting seemed easier, so I picked up a knife.

I looked down and wondered at how much trouble I was having directing my hands. "Really, really low blood sugar," I thought.

Then the phone rang across the room. The phone sits on a table beside a blue couch by the windows with the long view over the bay. I walked over, answered the phone, sat down, and began to talk. Something was funny with my speech. I was having trouble forming words. The person on the other end, my husband's daughter, noticed immediately that my speech was slurred. "Hang up and call 911," she said. She didn't say, "You might have had a stroke." I had no clue what was happening. I was still operating on the low blood sugar premise. I listened politely, but I didn't think it was a big deal, so I thanked her and hung up the phone. To humor her, I decided to dial the twenty-four-hour on-call nurse at my health plan, Kaiser Permanente. Of course the on-call nurse knew what might be going on. She immediately told me to call 911.

Feeling quite foolish, I woke my beloved husband, Bob, and called 911. We lived on a mountain and knew the paramedics at the fire station up the road from various disaster-planning activities in our neighborhood. The station was only three minutes from our house. In a very short while, paramedics I knew came up on the porch and in the door. They proceeded to start the drill I'd learned in my first-responder training, asking me the usual questions — starting with "What's your name? What's today's date? Where are you?" — all of which I answered easily, feeling more and more foolish. Then they called the ambulance to take me to the hospital.

Paramedics are wonderful. If I ran the world, paramedics would be paid more than the people who play professional sports.

As we waited for the ambulance, I was still thinking that this response was way, way over the top, and I was both scared and embarrassed. The ambulance came, bringing more paramedics with it. The new ones put me in a lift chair, carried me down the steps, and loaded me into the waiting ambulance. They wouldn't let me sit up. They insisted I lie down, and they took my blood pressure. One of them sat beside me the entire trip. I struck up a conversation with this paramedic, who like all the rest was a lovely person — friendly, warm, and professional. I thought that I would rather talk to him than think about how silly I felt, lying there in an ambulance with my beloved husband following behind in his car.

At the emergency room I was taken in right away and sent for a CAT scan. A little while later the doctor came in and said, "You have bleeding on your brain stem. You might die. But I think you'll be all right." I was fifty-five and fit, right? I didn't think I was going to die. I still didn't know that I'd had a stroke. All I concentrated on were the last words he'd said: ". . . you'll be all right." "Fine," I thought. "I'll be all right. Let's get out of here."

Fortunately, the doctor was wiser than I and insisted that I be admitted to the neurological intensive-care hospital an hour south of my house. This required another ambulance ride and another long stretch of following behind for my husband in his car.

At the new hospital, the neurologist told me that he would

have sent me home. Luckily for me, the emergency-room doctor at the first hospital had other ideas. After a long wait in the emergency room at this second hospital, I was admitted, placed in the neurological intensive-care ward, and given treatment to attempt to reduce the swelling in my brain. Brains don't like blood loose in the wrong place. The brain sees blood outside the veins, arteries, and capillaries as poison. Loose blood kills brain tissue, and the rest swells up in response to the injury. It's a good thing that I was in the hospital, because sometime after midnight, on May 4, I had another bleed, with the potential for ever more swelling and escalating damage.

Sometimes when people have hemorrhagic strokes, neurologists perform brain surgery to stop the bleeding. They don't like to do this with the brain stem. The brain stem is the old part of the brain. It's little. It's compact. It controls really important things like breathing and your heartbeat. Cutting it open can do more harm than good. Serious swelling and pressure on the part that regulates your heart or your lungs can make you dead. We could only pray that the bleeding was stopped and wouldn't start again.

Only enough blood to cover an area of roughly 2.7 centimeters in diameter got loose in my brain. That's not much, not much at all. But that little bit of blood in the wrong place, in that highly delicate brain stem, caused the following problems: My left arm was completely paralyzed. Most of my left leg was paralyzed. My trunk muscles wouldn't respond. I couldn't sit up. My right arm and leg responded to my thoughts of moving them, but they were wildly uncoordinated and wandered all over the place. My swallowing reflex was gone. I had to have a feeding tube inserted up my nose and down my throat. My speech was heavily slurred, and I had very little breath with which to speak. I was pretty hard to understand. My eyes wouldn't focus. My ability to control my emotional expression was shot. I either looked as if I were devoid of feeling or I laughed or cried uncontrollably — often both at once. I lost control of my bladder and my bowels, so I had to wear diapers, which was better than what happened later, when my ability to urinate on my own shut down for ten days and I had to be catheterized every six hours.

If you have never had a brain injury or a stroke (and I hope you never have and never will), you'll find that it's virtually impossible to imagine the depth of the injury and the overwhelming fatigue that accompanies it. You can see the obvious disabilities in people who've had strokes or other brain injuries. But what you can't see is the extraordinary effort it takes to do the smallest thing. What you can't see is the way the body responds to the attack on such a fundamental organ. The power of that fatigue is unlike anything I'd ever experienced; there's nothing even close.

So many problems were created from a little bit of blood in the wrong place. I'd received a real-world lesson in just how fragile bodies are. And now I was in the hospital, profoundly injured and disabled, and the lessons this experience would teach me began. I couldn't see them as lessons at first. I was struggling to stay alive. But nonetheless I was beginning to discover the power of transformation.

I was beginning to learn that it's not what happens to us

that matters, not even something as bad as a brain-stem stroke. What matters is how we deal with what happens to us. How we work with what is — whatever that might be — makes all the difference.

The rest of this book is about what I learned and how I apply these lessons to my whole life, not just to my recovery, which, by the way, has been remarkable. I'm aware of my continuing limitations, but most folks have no idea I had two strokes unless I tell them.

# CHAPTER TWO

## A Lifelong Dream

I SUPPOSE IT'S A GOOD THING that I had no idea how the transformative lessons of my life would unfold. If I'd known, I'd probably have locked myself in my room and thrown away the key. I sometimes jokingly remark to my friends that it used to be so hard to teach me important lessons that it took two strokes to get me to pay attention. I trust that you're considerably smarter and more teachable than I am.

The story of transformation starts, for me, with a lifelong dream. It starts with my beginning to reach for something I'd always wanted and hadn't acknowledged out loud, something I hadn't been willing to believe until then that I could take action to achieve.

Until shortly before the stroke, my life had been a series of episodes threaded together by work and marriage and children, not so different from many other lives. When I was in my midtwenties and getting a divorce, I went to work to support my two small boys. This was during the early 1970s in Atlanta, Georgia. Women in Atlanta in those days weren't expected to have careers. I was taught that my job was to get married, then have children and stay home with them. The

only career in the picture was supposed to be my husband's.
Not too many years had passed since my mother stopped
insisting that if you were going downtown you should be
wearing stockings, heels, and gloves.

I needed a job after my divorce, but I certainly had no
training for a career. Finding what I could, I went to work as
legal secretary and apprentice bookkeeper in a small law firm
in Atlanta. The firm had two offices and two lawyers. One
practiced litigation. The other practiced real estate. Another
legal secretary and I shared the open work space with the file
cabinets, typewriters, and copy machine. The law library, the
first room you saw as you entered the space, doubled as a conference room and was filled with impressive-looking books.
Unfortunately, my job included the ceaselessly boring task of
replacing loose-leaf pages in those books whenever new case
law was enacted.

I quickly figured out that I didn't like being a secretary.
I'm not all that fond of being told what to do. Lacking flexibility and with little in the way of formal skills, I followed the
path in front of me, teaching myself to be a paralegal with a
focus on commercial real estate simply because that's what
the lawyer I worked for did. I took a course on law at a state
college, learned how to do title searches and closings, and
then went to work for a big law firm. The main advantage of
working at a big firm, as I saw it, was that I could learn new
things and maybe have some small say in what I did.

At the big firm I was given an office. The office had been
a closet before I moved in, and the desk spanned the entire
width. Fortunately the closet had two doors. I came in the

first door if I wanted to sit behind the desk. If something fell off the front of the desk, I went out the door into the hall and opened the second door to get it. But it was my very own office, and I loved it.

Working for the big firm was satisfying for a couple of years, until one day I realized that I'd learned enough to catch the mistakes of some of the lawyers around me. I thought about this and looked at their offices, their lifestyles, and their salaries. I said to myself, "They're making ten times as much money as I am." This didn't seem like a reasonable proposition to me. I felt as capable as they were, although I knew I lacked their formal training. Going to law school wasn't an option for me, and by that time I'd decided that I didn't really want to be a lawyer anyway. What was I to do next?

Still following the path in front of me, I looked around and discovered an opportunity to work for a client of my current law firm who was in the real estate development business, with a specialty of creating neighborhood shopping centers. These centers are familiar to most people. Neighborhood shopping centers have grocery stores, sometimes discount department stores, and big drugstores, and the small businesses so many people go to — the cleaners, card shops, and restaurants. As with any other commercial property, neighborhood shopping centers need to be planned, financed, built, leased, and managed. There was plenty of work to do, and I was eager to do it. This new job brought me many more new things to learn.

And so began the eighteen years I was to spend in commercial real estate property operations doing management, construction, leasing, marketing, and all the other multitudes of tasks that particular business brings with it. Being a jill-of-all-trades appealed to me, and I took to my new world. Once in it, I discovered that this was also a world in which, at last, I could have more say in what I did and what choices were made. That appealed to me too. Staying in Atlanta, getting remarried, and managing large, multiuse properties, then moving to the West Coast while continuing to raise my children — these were busy times.

On the West Coast, I ran diverse properties in four states, got another divorce, went to graduate school to earn an MBA, and met and married my third husband, Bob, the love of my life. With my MBA in hand — formal training at last — I left the real estate business and began consulting for small businesses and nonprofits.

I had always followed my nose. I'd been happy and good at what I did, but despite it all I'd never had the courage to reach for what my heart really wanted to do. Hidden in all that activity — all that working in the business world, making a living, and raising my children — was the secret avocation of my heart, making art. I loved to paint and draw. My inner, unspoken wish was to illustrate a children's book.

Throughout the years I hadn't had much time for drawing and painting, but I made what little time I could. I would draw when the boys were asleep, their sweet innocent faces peaceful and serene. I reached for paper and pencils whenever I could capture a few minutes to myself, whenever the demands on my time slowed down enough for a breath.

On the West Coast, the boys grew up and moved on with

their lives. Though I was working sixty to seventy hours a week, which required traveling to all the properties I was managing, when I could find the time I began to take occasional small art courses in the adult education section of a local community college. I relished the thrill of working with models and charcoal, standing in front of an easel, able for an hour to lose myself completely in the curve of a leg or the shape of a face, as the soft sounds of the charcoal against the paper whispered in my ear.

The rest of my life always called me back from the charcoal to a flurry of activity. I'd finished my MBA, married Bob, and begun the consulting business all at the same time. Bob was considerably older than I was when we married. A remarkable man in many ways, he was also the kindest person I've ever known. Bob had a series of successful careers beginning with plumbing, which he learned from his father as a boy growing up in Chicago. When I'd talk about my property management experience, Bob would delight in reminding me that he still had his plumbing license. After high school Bob earned a scholarship to college and law school and became a lawyer, but he decided that he didn't like the law and went into business instead, first as a consultant and then as an executive in the envelope industry. Throughout his life, Bob's fascination with people and generosity of heart led him to study psychology and spiritual philosophy and to put his energy behind various people and organizations over the years to give back to the world — what he called "paying his dues." His passion, though, was for travel. At any opportunity he would visit some new part of the world, and he had friends in surprising places. Marrying Bob was one of the greatest blessings of my life.

Bob, being much wiser than I was, invited me to include more ease in my life, to breathe and slow down enough to notice more of the life around me. I remember walking on the mountain one day after I married Bob and seeing the wildflowers in bloom. By that time I'd lived in the San Francisco Bay Area for seven years. But while walking a meandering rock-strewn path, I realized that in all the time I'd been on the West Coast, I'd never before noticed those flowers in bloom. Looking at the delicate wild irises with their pale yellows and subtle lavenders was a revelation.

Bob encouraged me in many things, and most of all he urged me to listen to my heart. With my consulting business came more flexibility. I gathered my dreams and my courage, and with Bob's support and the memory of the wild irises, I enrolled in an art college part-time. I was the oldest student in the class, but I was filled with the intention of taking all the rigorous courses I would need, one at a time, and learning all I could to reach for my secret dream.

Life has a funny way of proceeding at its own pace, sometimes with little regard for the orderly timing we imagine. One of my consulting clients was a publisher. I'd taken just a few courses in the art college when one day my client called me and started talking about a children's book she was considering publishing. I was sitting downstairs at the long wooden desk that hangs on the wall when she called. With the portable phone in my hand, I got up to walk around as I talked. The walking must have relaxed me and lowered my guard, because somewhere out of the depths of my desire the words of my dream came out of my mouth. I asked her if I could illustrate the book. I was astonished at myself, but she actually said she would think about it. Two weeks later she called me back. I will remember that moment forever. I remained fairly calm on the phone when she said that, yes, she would take a chance on me and let me illustrate the book, but by the time I made it halfway up the stairs to tell my husband I was yelling wildly. I couldn't believe my good fortune.

I was illustrating a children's book! Me. What a wonder! I hadn't yet finished the art courses and I had to learn a lot of things quickly, but on-the-job learning wasn't new to me. I'd been doing it all my life. Linda, the publisher; her daughter Jan, the writer; and I met to scope out the characters: a family of bears, with a mother, father, sister, and brother, and their two pets, a dog and a cat. We talked about the locations, inside a house, outside a house, and the time of day, from morning to night. I began to work with the text. Pretty soon, with some supportive coaching from Linda, who had worked with other first-time illustrators, I produced the storyboard drawings. These are little drawings that roughly tell the visual story in response to the writer's words.

Another wonder. Linda liked my concepts. Then came the finish drawings — the big ones that show all the detail. A few corrections, and I (that means me — I still couldn't believe this was happening) was turned loose to paint. There are thirty-two pages in a standard children's book, and this publisher likes double-page spreads, full-bleed. That means one painting with no borders (a full-bleed illustration goes all the way to the edge of the page) for each two-page spread, plus one for the cover — a total of seventeen paintings. This is not the simplest way to illustrate a book for a beginner, but I was learning how to do it.

And so I began to paint. Standing in my funny, funky studio space with clear plastic sheets taped on the windows to seal in the heat, and bare, scuffed wooden floors, I experimented with approaches to the painting. It took nine tries to find a style and get the first illustration right. I certainly could have used more of those art courses. Finally I produced an illustration I was willing to show, and Linda told me that she loved it.

I had found my style and knew what I needed to do. Oh my, I was on a roll! I'd get up every morning and go to the studio. Carefully putting the first painting where I could refer to it, I finished the next painting and started on the one after that. I was really getting the hang of this.

Just as I was working on the third illustration, one of our neighbors died. I knew Howard. He was a favorite of everyone in our neighborhood on the mountain, a central figure in every get-together. Howard could talk with all kinds of people and make them feel that they were special and the complete focus of his attention. With a mischievous twinkle in his eye and his generous heart, Howard brought a smile to everybody's face.

The neighborhood wanted to hold a grand celebration of Howard's life. Plans were under way for a community memorial, with food and storytelling. There was much discussion about how we could best honor Howard's open, playful spirit. Then someone came up with a great idea. Howard loved kites.

Why not make a kite with Howard's picture on it to fly off the bluff next to the community center where the party would be held? Everyone could stand outside and help to send Howard up in the air soaring above the mountain he was so much a part of and so loved. Neighbors met this idea with great enthusiasm, and some came to me and asked me to draw a picture of Howard that they could blow up, print out on large architectural paper, and use to fashion a kite. I agreed. People on the mountain still talk about that party and Howard's kite.

This is Howard:

The drawing of Howard done, I went back to work on the book and finished the third illustration. Then I started on the fourth. This one didn't seem to be going as well as the first three. I felt a little more tentative, a little awkward. Little did I know at the time just how awkward I would become. Struggling with the fourth illustration, feeling tired and frustrated,

I suggested to Bob that we have a quiet evening and go to bed early.

As I lay down in my bed to go to sleep that night, I had no idea that it would be the night that so fundamentally changed my life.

And now here I was in the neurological intensive care ward, with the steady, clicking noises of the feeding-tube machine as the background music to my nights and days. My dream, so I thought, had been shattered. I spent ten days in that hospital, ten days of experiencing profound helplessness — being fed by a tube, having my diapers changed, needing someone else to clean me, move me, handle me, dress me.

For several days I got worse, then I stabilized. Just before I left the hospital, the doctors were able to remove the feeding tube. I still couldn't swallow normally, especially not ordinary water. To slow the process of swallowing, they put thickener in the water. I know intellectually and medically that this is a good idea. But, honestly, it's hard to imagine anything more obnoxious than having to drink a glass of water that has turned into a gelatinous, mealy glob in your mouth.

My left side was still paralyzed. I couldn't sit up. I couldn't walk. My right hand shook and swung so much I could do very little with it. I'd been active and engaged, living my dream, and now I felt truly helpless. My doctor would come in to see me and say in a voice so cheery that it made my teeth hurt, "You're so ready for rehab!" I had no earthly idea what she meant, but bless her heart, she, like the emergency-room doctor, knew what I needed, and arranged to have me admitted to the rehabilitation hospital as soon as I was discharged from the hospital I was in.

Another ambulance ride and another long follow in the car by my distraught husband took us to Vallejo, an hour from home in another direction. I remember being wheeled down the corridors of the rehab hospital on a gurney, looking at the ceiling tiles go by, with no idea what rehab might be like, but thinking that somehow once I was in rehab everything would be okay and the doctors would fix me. How little I knew then. And now the lessons of transformation began.

# CHAPTER THREE

## *Taking Responsibility*

I WAS BROUGHT TO MY ROOM and put in the bed in the corner by the window. Four corners, four beds. My part of the room contained a bed, a tray table, a small TV on a swing arm that came over the bed, a phone, a curtain, a little dresser, a counter by the window with a small sink that the nurses used, and a bulletin board on the wall. This corner was to be my home for as long as I stayed in rehab.

A good rehab hospital does many things. The first is to jump-start your recovery, and the second is to bring you face-to-face, no-holds-barred, with just how profoundly disabled you are. Lying in the hospital, even with as little as I could do, I had no real idea of the extent of what I had lost. That knowledge came when I reached rehab. In the hospital, I was passive. In rehab, I was fitted for a wheelchair, shown the way to the gym and the other departments, and told it would be up to me to find my way to them several times a day. Driving a wheelchair with one side paralyzed and the other shaking is not the easiest form of locomotion, but it was the only one I had. I kept veering sideways when I pushed with my right hand; I wobbled down the hall until I learned to compensate with my right foot.

I was still holding the thought that I'd come to rehab, stay there until I was functional, and go home when I could cope. I wasn't really sure what that might mean, but I certainly wasn't prepared to learn that I would be sent home in two and a half weeks. I now know that the average stay in a rehab hospital in the United States is sixteen to eighteen days. Sometimes, if you're lucky, your stay gets extended by another week. Many times, if you have poor medical coverage or none at all, there's no rehab for you. I was one of the lucky ones.

Yikes. I couldn't stand up on my own. Walking was a joke. I was so spastic that even when I tried to use a walker, the therapist by my side had to be ready to catch me at any moment when I started to pitch over sideways. And I was going to be sent home in two and a half weeks? I was terrified — numb. I didn't know what to think.

Wobbling down the hall in my wheelchair, I came to the corner where my day would begin. To the left the corridor led to the rehab gym. To the right it led to the patient dining room. I took a deep mental breath, turned the corner to the left, and proceeded to the rehab gym. My first sight of it with my unfocused eyes was bewildering: It was a huge space with therapists and patients coming and going; raised mats; pieces of equipment unlike any I'd ever seen, designed to do things I couldn't imagine; objects piled in corners; and a whole series of parallel bars taking up one-quarter of the room, lined up in what looked like some kind of a maze. I didn't know what to make of it.

Today I wish I had a picture of my first time between the parallel bars in the gym. Then, I wouldn't have wanted anyone to see me, although of course the rehab gym was filled with people. The patients were too busy with their own problems to notice mine. The therapists had seen it all before.

When a leg becomes paralyzed, the foot becomes unresponsive, the ankle joint is slack, and the toes don't lift. Before I was fitted with a hard plastic brace to hold up my foot, my gait therapist (as in walking gait), Julia, stabilized my left foot and ankle with an elastic bandage to keep my toes from dragging. She placed me upright between the bars as I held on with my right hand and Julia wrapped herself around me like a pretzel while she attempted to get my left hip to come forward, my knee to bend, and my toes not to drag as she encouraged my shaky right side to start a walking motion. My immobile left hand was balanced on the bar and sort of slid along with the rest of me as Julia pulled, pushed, and half carried me forward. Remember my slurred speech and swallowing difficulties? Along with them came little control of the face muscles on the left side of my face. So on top of everything else, I was drooling on the poor kid. And I was going home?

Nobody was talking to me about what abilities, if any, I could recover. Nobody said a word. All they did was work with me. This wasn't meant to be cruel or intentionally obscure. The truth, which I didn't know then, is that nobody knows. Recovering from a stroke is not like healing a broken leg. It's a whole lot more like life. There are no guarantees. Nobody knows the outcome. The doctors were not giving us platitudes or certainties. Working in that gym, I was learning that nobody, but nobody, was going to fix me. Many people would help me, but nobody could kiss it and make it all better for me.

So who else was there? It was a simple process of elimination. I realized there was only one person left. That person was me. Gradually I came to see that the person who would make the most difference in what happened in my recovery and my ability to find a new life was sitting in that wheelchair figuring out how to steer straight with one side paralyzed.

While I was in rehab, the hospital arranged for a home visit. That sounded nice: Go home. See the trees. See the cat. Sleep in my own bed. But that's not really the purpose of the home visit. Facing my disability in rehab was merely an introduction to facing my disability in the context of my house on the mountain. Everything in rehab is on one floor designed for wheelchairs. Highly competent people are available twenty-four hours a day to help you.

But I live in a little two-story house on a mountain. Getting into the house requires going up steps. The staircase between the two floors curves and has a minimum of handrails, and those it has are on the left side — the side of me that wasn't moving. The house and garage are separated by a sloped gravel parking area. The bedroom isn't big enough for a wheelchair. And these are but a few of the challenges.

When I went home for my first home visit, I had a twenty-four-hour Foley catheter. A Foley catheter is a tube inserted in the urethra, connected to a bag to collect urine. I couldn't urinate on my own. I was strapped to a bag. How difficult was that going to be at home? My left hand didn't work. I couldn't catheterize myself. Keeping a semipermanent catheter in is not only cumbersome; it can be dangerous. It's all too easy to get a serious infection from a Foley catheter. In the hospital, the nurses would catheterize me every six hours and drain my bladder.

I realized that my very first priority was to learn how to pee again. No doctor or therapist was going to teach me that one. I asked for advice. I forced fluids. I talked to my body. I learned that my bowel and bladder sphincters operated from the same part of the brain. I encouraged everything. And the night I came back from that first home visit, to my utmost joy, the dam finally broke and gradually I began to get the function back. To this day, I remain grateful for that one.

In the rehab hospital, I had a card that hung from the side of my wheelchair. The card listed my appointments with the physical therapist, the speech therapist, the occupational therapist, and my doctor. Each appointment was color-coded, blue for PT, yellow for speech, green for OT, and red for the physician's office. The floor of the rehab hospital had stripes on it. The stripes corresponded in color to the colors of the appointments and laid out the directional paths I needed to follow in my wheelchair to get to the various departments.

Strokes are confusing. Having cues helps. But when I went home, there were no cues — no PT, speech, and OT departments, no appointments, no stripes on the floor of my house. Looking at my house on my first visit home, I realized that it was a pretty good thing I'd never been fond of other people telling me what to do, because there wasn't going to be anybody there to do that now.

I didn't know, and couldn't know at that point, that my

recovery was going to take several years. In fact, stroke recovery is something that continues all your life. I had yet to discover that I had a long haul ahead of me, but I was beginning to see that all of my therapists, as wonderful as they were, could only give me a jump start. The rest was up to me. I was beginning to see that I was, and am, the key to my own recovery.

But what exactly did that mean? I agree it was a good thing that I liked taking responsibility for things and that I was willing to take on challenges I didn't immediately know how to solve, but what did it really mean to be the key to my own recovery? How could I do that?

I would have to call on the skills I already had. We learn many skills during the course of our lives, and we often think the skills apply only to the place where we learned them. In fact, our skills transcend the content of a situation, and if we're willing, we can apply them anywhere. I was a professional problem solver. Problems are the day-to-day fare of property managers and business consultants. What else would we have to do if we didn't have problems to solve? A customer with a roof that leaks when it rains? Track down the roofer or maybe even the builder who built the building or the architect who designed it. Another customer doesn't have the rent this month? Work with him or her to create a payment plan. I came to realize that I could apply these problem-solving skills to my recovery.

I was shifting from a rigorous daily schedule of exercise and challenges to unstructured time at home. That was a problem unless I solved it. Human beings respond to structure. We organize ourselves around specific times, goals, rules, and interactions. While I might often feel irritated and constrained by rules, left without any structure I have a tendency to get disorganized and have a hard time getting things done.

I would have to create my own schedule at home, figure out when I would work, when I would rest, when I would eat. I was leaving an equipped rehab gym. How could I turn my house, my every task, from brushing my teeth to going to the bathroom, into an opportunity for rehab? I had problem-solving skills, but before I could use them there were some other things I needed to know. How would I start?

Most of the people I've met, including me, take a while to get this lesson. I didn't realize all at once that I would need to take charge of my recovery. The understanding developed as I worked in the gym and thought about my home and how I would deal with leaving rehab.

Frank got it immediately. I met Frank one night when I was speaking at the rehab hospital last year. Speaking is something I've been doing on a regular basis since July of 2005. It's a privilege to spend time with people who are seeking ways to help themselves recover.

Frank was eighty-three when I met him. He'd had a stroke that left him with his left side paralyzed, trouble with speech, and trouble with sitting up. I talked with Frank for a while, then went back to his room to see some photos of his earlier life. I listened while Frank told stories. He had been a gunner at seventeen in World War II in a very famous plane. I can't tell you which plane because then you could find out who Frank is and I want to preserve his privacy, but it was famous. Frank had also been part of a crew who had brought a plane back so badly shot up that the tail nearly fell off. Frank had been shot down in a jungle, then rescued by a local. He promptly became a resistance fighter for the next part of the war. Facing problems was what Frank had done his whole life.

Frank knows more about the power of taking charge of whatever situation he faces than I ever will. To Frank, recovering from a stroke was simply another challenge in a life of working with whatever hand he was dealt. Frank was using a wheelchair when I met him. He had every intention of walking again and getting back the use of his hand and speaking clearly. By the time he left the rehab hospital he was on his feet walking, and his hand and his speech were coming back. Frank wasted no time in getting to work. From the beginning he was ready to transform his experience.

I wasn't as ready to begin transforming my experience as Frank was. My skills were not as focused as his. In my case, I needed more steps in the process. I needed to start at the beginning to be able to put my problem-solving skills to work. And starting at the beginning turned out to be the next lesson I learned.

# CHAPTER FOUR

## *Affecting Your Own Life*

A S I LAY IN MY BED TOO TIRED to make any more effort, I would think, "Why me?" I'd had no risk factors for a stroke. I was fit. I was healthy. Why me? I reviewed my life, looking for the guilt, looking for the fault, looking for any explanation to account for what had happened to me. Somebody, something, somewhere must be to blame. If I could only find something to blame, I thought I would feel better.

From a distance of seven years, that view seems a bit obscure. How would finding something to blame make me feel better? How would it restore movement in my left hand? But for a time I was stuck in that question. Round and round and round went my head. I thought, "I was a good kid. I was decent. I was kind to my husband. The cat liked me. Why me?"

Was the stroke morally justified? Did I deserve it? I wasn't a bad person. I had integrity. I was doing good work for the world. I was illustrating a children's book, for heaven's sake, not planning evil deeds or hurting other people. Why me?

There's a fundamental problem with the "Why me?" question, even though almost all of us, except maybe Frank, ask it. The question simply doesn't go anywhere. It has no answer. It isn't designed to have an answer. We ask ourselves this question to perpetuate the fantasy that life is fair. We hold on to the view that if we just do everything "right," nothing bad will ever happen to us. Somehow we're going to be the exception to the rule. Everybody else will suffer and die, but we want to believe that we're cleverer than all the rest and somehow we'll be spared. Or we'll simply not *think* about it, and what we pretend isn't happening won't reach out and touch us. Given that our efforts didn't work this time, we believe that if we could only get an answer to the "Why me?" question, we could make absolutely sure something bad will never happen again.

Sorry, but I had to learn that life doesn't come that way. The strokes taught me that it wasn't a matter of *if* something was going to happen to me. It was simply a matter of *when* and *what*. If nothing else, I was certainly going to die. Much of the time we'd all rather not believe it, but it's true. And it's fairly likely that somewhere between being born and dying, no matter how hard we try, we'll experience some kind of suffering along the way. "Why me?" is a question without an answer.

One of the people at the rehab hospital where I work a lot these days says that she tells people who say they have no risk factors for a stroke that they're forgetting something. As long as you have a brain, she says, you have a risk factor for either a stroke or some other kind of brain injury. The risk of brain injury comes with having a brain. We all have them. We won't all get brain injuries, thank goodness, but we all bear the risk.

When I was in rehab, moving any part of my body took all the strength I had. I spent six hours a day in therapy five days a week, and half a day on Saturdays. I volunteered for extra sessions whenever I could get them. I was tired from working as hard as I could, and I simply didn't have the energy to waste on circular questions without answers.

What could I do? I realized that I had a choice. I could stop wasting energy. I could let go of the fantasy and move on to a different question, one that just might have an answer. I could keep on treading that endless circle of the "Why me?" question, or I could find another question to ask. The question I began to ask was this: *Now that this has happened to me, what am I going to do about it?*

This was a question I could work with. My strokes had happened. I couldn't make the strokes not happen. The blood was there in the wrong place. Asking "Why me?" or even "Why did this happen?" hadn't helped me. I'm not suggesting here that if some of us have contributed to our risk factors by refusing to treat our high blood pressure or any other medical condition known to increase the risk of stroke that we shouldn't do something in the future to decrease our risk. That's pretty self-evident. Or if it's not, we all might consider thinking about why not. Simple advice: If we're hurting ourselves, we need to try to find a way to stop.

On the other hand, I *am* suggesting that using precious energy to ask pointless questions and focusing on our misery isn't going to get us better. Problems are solved by looking for solutions, not by crying out how unfair it is that we have been given a problem. Stroke recovery is a problem to be solved, not a statement of our moral fitness. My strokes didn't happen because my mother had failed to love me enough. They didn't happen because I "deserved" this fate for some dreadful misdeed. They simply happened.

As long as I was trying to blame myself or someone or something else, I was preventing myself from taking charge of my own recovery. I was standing (well, at that point metaphorically) in my own way. And so I stopped asking "Why me?"

Stopping the circular, wasteful motion of "Why me?" made a little space in my heart and my energy. Into that space came the opportunity to pay attention to the impact of neuroplasticity.

## NEUROPLASTICITY

As recently as 2002, when I had my strokes, many doctors were still saying, "You have six months to make your recovery. If you don't get better within six months, you might have incremental improvements, but that will be it." This terribly destructive, self-fulfilling, and amazingly inaccurate view still persists in some corners. If I had a giant view eraser, I would spend the rest of my life eradicating that idea from every corner of the world. It simply isn't true. And it has done more harm to stroke survivors than you can imagine.

This misguided view stems from the old notion that the brain is like a car engine, a system of fixed parts. Current brain research has recently amply demonstrated that the brain is not like this at all. If you have all the normal sensory and motor systems and all the brain formations humans generally come with, parts of your brain will specialize. Your brain will dedicate one part for hearing, another for vision, and another for speech. But the brain is a dynamic, ever-changing, ever-remapping process, always ready to use itself as fully and efficiently as possible. That's what's known as *neuroplasticity* in action.

If you lose your hearing or your vision, the parts of the brain dedicated to those functions don't simply sit idle and empty. Brains are, biologically, expensive real estate. Leaving them vacant is wasteful. Your body will find other uses for your brain tissue. The wonderful thing is that this process is going on every minute, not just turning on once in a while. Your brain is constantly performing a self-check, evaluating the usefulness of itself.

What's also wonderfully true is that if a part of your brain is injured, you may be able to recruit some other part to take over the function the injured part used to do. This is evident everywhere. I've seen it time and time and time again. Long before I heard the term *neuroplasticity*, I learned this lesson by living it. Every day I learn this lesson again from the stroke survivors I meet. But it was hard for a while to convince some people, even some well-meaning medical people, that this is true. All too often, those of us who managed to get a lot of function back were considered the exceptions to the rule, the miracles. I don't want to be a miracle. I want to be evidence to somebody else that transformation is possible.

Believe me, I jumped for joy when Dr. Norman Doidge's book, *The Brain That Changes Itself*, became available. Sitting on an airplane as I flew to Atlanta, I read this book and grinned from ear to ear. The research was now here. Neuroplasticity has been measured, demonstrated, and scientifically validated, and the information has become available to all of us.

Researchers are working with stroke patients. At a national stroke conference I attended in 2007, I met a medical researcher from Wake Forest University in North Carolina who conducted a study using MRI imaging of the brains of stroke survivors up to twenty-three months postinjury. A brilliant rehabilitation technique researched and made widely available by Edward Taub called *constraint-induced movement therapy* produced clear evidence under the imaging that new, uninjured parts of the brain were firing up to do the work required.

I didn't have all this theory to back me up when I was first injured. I had a little bit of knowledge along with real-world practice and emerging experience. For a long time I had to rely on my powers of observation and my general stubbornness and unwillingness to believe that I would have only a limited time to get better. Initially much of that practice and observation happened in the rehab gym.

The rehab gym has a free space in the center. We patients would wheel ourselves in and line up, as best we could with our various limitations, in the middle of the room waiting for our therapists to come and get us and lead us to our time with the appointed equipment, whatever that might be. As we were lined up, sometimes we would talk a little with one another and watch as patients of all sizes and ages went through their routines. We all had different appointments during the day with various physical therapists, depending on the nature of our injuries and our ability to work.

In my case, I had three daily appointments in the gym. Each day I would see my lead physical therapist, Erwin. The rest of my life, no matter how long it might be, can't possibly contain enough days to experience all the gratitude I have for Erwin. Erwin organized my PT treatment plan and worked with me individually. I also had an appointment with Julia, my sweet and patient gait therapist, and then there were the mat appointments. The mat therapists varied. They were all great, talented, and kind. They taught me many things. They couldn't help the fact that I hated mats.

Mats involve group work. They are repetitive exercises designed to build strength and coordination. Three or four patients are lined up on a raised mat, off the floor, on legs, rather like a very large, low table. The first thing you have to learn in order to do mat work is safe movement in and out of your wheelchair and onto the mat. The instructions are precise. It's important to learn them to be able to transfer yourself safely. It's scary when you have no confidence that even with help you can be momentarily on your feet, turn, feel for the edge, and sit.

The appointments with Erwin and Julia entailed a constant, moment-to-moment interaction with each therapist. These therapists became like extensions of my body, guiding it, stimulating it, helping it get where it needed to go. With them, I could experience possibility. On the mat, however, I was on my own, lying there side by side with other patients as I tried to follow instructions.

Bridging is a trunk-strengthening exercise. Having learned it, I still do bridging, although I'm much better at it than I was then. At the time it was a struggle. Most of the work was being done by my right leg, as shaky as it was. My left was largely along for the ride, and my left foot had to be wedged in place to keep my left knee bent. The object is to slowly raise and then even more slowly lower your bottom off the mat and then back onto the mat. I wobbled. I shook. I had the barest control. And I had to do it over and over and over again in sets of ten.

On the mat there was nothing to distract me from my miserable thoughts. I inevitably compared myself with other patients who could "do it better" than I could, which left me feeling even more helpless. But on the mat I was learning to work even if I couldn't see the success of what I was doing. I didn't like mats, but learning to work without an assurance of success proved to be a very powerful tool in my recovery.

I now know that walking is not so much performed by the legs but by the trunk muscles. These are the muscles of the back, the abdomen, and the chest. Surprising, isn't it? But it's true. Try strengthening your core, and see how much more easily you'll walk. My core was weak, and my trunk muscle control was poor. I needed a lot of strengthening. I lay on the mat thinking about how fit I'd been. How easily I had walked. But there was bridging to do. Day after day, I lay on that mat and did the bridging exercises.

During my first few days at the rehab hospital, I was strapped to my wheelchair with a seat belt. I felt like a little kid in a car seat. It wasn't easy to accept the fact that without the strap I might slide out of the chair, like a baby who hasn't learned how to sit up. But with weak, uncoordinated trunk muscles, this result was likely. Bridging changed that. After many days of spending time on the mat, I could sit up on my own without the seat belt.

It wasn't that my muscles had suddenly stopped being strong when I had my strokes. My muscles weren't much different than they had been ten days earlier — a little weaker from inactivity but not all that much. What had changed was my brain's communication with my muscles. What I was bringing back was the link between my trunk and my conscious decision to do something.

In his book *Musicophilia*, the famous neurologist Oliver Sacks tells us that if a musician temporarily loses the use of a finger, the area of the brain devoted to operating that finger shrinks. And if the musician exercises one finger more than the others, the area devoted to that specific finger expands more than the others. This is the way the brain works. When we put our effort and intention on something, the brain responds.

If I wanted to regain the use of my body, I would have to recruit new brain tissue to take over from the injured parts. The more I worked, the greater the likelihood that expensive brain real estate would be diverted to accomplishing what I was trying to accomplish.

I now know that within the limits of our anatomy and experience, we're the architects of our abilities. Neuroplasticity can create amazing opportunities for change.

Some changes are harder to make than others. Speech-center injuries are among the most difficult to work with. I have a friend named Rita Martin. I met her two and a half

years ago. Rita is one of the most remarkable people I know.
Rita had a stroke in 1996, nearly thirteen years ago — a left
cerebral hemorrhage. Rita's speech center was wiped out,
gone. She had no ability to speak. She could think, but she
couldn't say anything. The speech therapists told her that
with extensive speech therapy she might, just might, be able
to say yes and no someday. Rita didn't give up. Rita never
gives up.

For a year and a half, Rita didn't talk, not a word. And
once she began to talk, her speech was aphasic. *Nonfluent
aphasia* is the ability to think a word without the ability to say
the word you think. You think apple. You say "window" or
"road" or something else totally unrelated, or only vaguely
related, to what you're thinking. Amazingly frustrating,
right?

In response to that frustration, many people give up the
attempt to talk. Remember what happens with neuroplasticity when you stop trying? No effort, no brain real estate
devoted to the task. As I said, Rita never gives up. When I
met her in 2007, Rita could already carry on a great conversation and she has continued to improve since. Sometimes it
takes her a while to find the way to the word. She may say,
"How do you say...?" before she finds it. Some days are better than others. But Rita isn't finished yet. She's still working
on her speech.

When I first had my strokes, I had no idea that I had the
power, the built-in biological ability, to become the instrument of my own recovery. I'd never thought about my life
that way. At first I nourished my own personal version of the

"I've been pushed around by life and it isn't my fault" story. It's one thing not to like being told what to do. It's another thing altogether to take real responsibility for the process of my own life. But the stroke was offering me this lesson in a way that I couldn't avoid. What I did, and the choices I made, registered in my brain tissue. In the rehab gym I could see in myself and in other patients that change was possible. If I'd decided not to work and to just sit and feel sorry for myself, nothing would have changed. I'd still be unable to move. I watched and saw that those who worked at it seemed to make the most changes. Those who were passive seemed to make fewer changes, no matter how hard their therapists tried.

Deciding to be the architect of my future was not such a simple decision. I didn't just lie on the mat and in great clarity of mind and heart say, "No problem. I'll do this." There was a lot more I needed to learn first, which brought me to the next lesson.

# CHAPTER FIVE

## *Facing Forward*

WHILE I WAS IN THE REHAB HOSPITAL, a friend, my next-door neighbor, Marge, came to see me. Marge is a wonderful artist. We had often drawn together in a figure-drawing class in the neighborhood community center. She thought I would likely be missing drawing and painting. People really had no idea how profoundly disabled I was.

Marge walked into my room with a pad of paper and some chalk pastels in her hands. I love pastels. Before I began to work in watercolor, I delighted in painting with pastels. They don't work well for book illustrations because the original paintings are sent by my publisher to the printer to be wrapped around a drum scanner, and pastels will smear. Watercolor is an ideal medium for drum scanners. It won't smear, but it's flexible enough to bend. However, the colors of pastels make my blood sing and my mouth water in a way that watercolors never can — especially the reds. No medium creates more color intensity on the page than pastels. In any other circumstance, I would have been delighted at such a gift.

That day I was heartsick. Seeing the pastels and the paper made me sad. What was I going to do with them? I thanked Marge and visited with her for a while. I didn't touch the pastels or the paper. When Marge left, I asked the CNA (certified nursing assistant) to put the gift away in the little dresser beside the bed, which she did. And I forgot about it, or tried to.

Sundays in the rehab hospital were generally quiet. If you weren't home Saturday night into Sunday for a home visit, or if nobody came to see you on Sunday, there wasn't much to do. No therapy on Sundays. I couldn't read. My eyes wouldn't focus well enough. I could watch TV, more or less, but usually I didn't find anything that interested me on the three channels available in the hospital. So one Sunday I was sitting in my wheelchair, wanting something to distract me from my miserable thoughts, and I decided I would take out the paper and the chalks. Maybe I could draw after all.

I leaned forward. Carefully, carefully. It wasn't so long ago that I'd been given permission to stop using the seat belt, and I had no intention of falling out of the wheelchair and finding myself strapped in again. My left arm was still inert, so I reached into the drawer with my shaky right hand and pulled out the paper and the chalks. I balanced them carefully on my lap.

Taking a breath, alone behind the curtains surrounding my bed, I began to try to draw. I worked as hard as I could and did the best that I could do. This is what I drew:

When I saw what I could do, I cried. Sitting there in my wheelchair, my heart broke. Grief and fear overwhelmed me. Looking at what I'd drawn, I realized that I had no idea if I would ever walk again, much less if I would ever draw and paint again.

Right there, in the midst of those tears, I began to understand that I would have to let go of the book and my dream. I had to learn to walk. I had to find a way back to my left arm and hand. I had to find out if I would be able to focus my eyes again and see clearly. I had to find out if I could cope at my house, or be able to drive again, or cook a meal, or tie my shoes.

I would later read in one of Rabbi David Wolpe's books, *Making Loss Matter*, "The answer lies not in return but in transformation." By the time I read this book, I'd learned this lesson by living it. I agree with the rabbi. As Wolpe tells us, there's no return. We can't go back to what we have been. We can only go forward to what we can be. In that room with the drawing in my hand, I had no idea what I could be, but I knew I needed all my energy to find out. I couldn't afford to spend time and energy worrying about the book. I had to let go of my dream. And I cried.

I frantically wondered how best to think about what was in front of me. I remembered that my beloved friend and mentor Stanley Keleman, a wise and gifted psychologist who developed what he calls *formative psychology*, had been attempting to teach me for years that the body is always re-forming itself. In this way, the body is a lot like the brain. We like to think of ourselves as fixed, immutable, solid. This muddled thinking pattern is similar to the one that leads to the "Why me?" question. We believe we're a sure thing, something that doesn't change, or at least something that doesn't change much. The untruth of this is remarkably evident if we pay attention. Whoever we are today, we're physically different from who we were ten years ago, or even five years ago. And if we look closely enough, we can see that we're different from who we were just one minute ago.

Stanley teaches that not only do we change through life with the process of growing and aging — growing taller, maturing, growing older and possibly shorter, sometimes heavier, sometimes lighter — we also change because of the ways we use ourselves. If I'm feeling helpless and overburdened, I'm likely to stand stoop-shouldered and collapsed. If I'm feeling strong and confident, I'm likely to stand with my chest high and my shoulders back. How we form our lives is largely a result of how we use ourselves to make that happen.

This changing ourselves through the course of our lives is beneficial. It's how we grow, how we absorb the lessons we learn, how we become wiser and more full of life. The more we honor this process and don't try to stop it, the fuller our lives can be. Thanks to Stanley, I already had some idea of this concept when I had the stroke, and he promptly reminded me of it when he talked to me as I lay in my hospital bed. I was changing anyway. The stroke had caused abrupt change, but according to Stanley there was no reason to believe that the way I was immediately poststroke was any more immutable than any other state I'd ever been in. We're all processes, not things. We're living beings, not bicycles.

I'd changed. That I knew for certain, but I can't say that I was all that keen on the little I could do to avoid the lesson of change in that moment. Denial is so comfortable. I would have been really happy to hang out in denial for a long time, pretending that my life was not turned upside down. But how could I? Even when I was sleeping in my bed, my inability to roll over and sleep on my side made the fact that I'd changed unavoidable.

I couldn't avoid knowing that I had changed and changed abruptly. I certainly wanted to change some more — to not stay the way I was — but how could I maximize the possibility for further change? How could I help myself? As I've said before, letting go of the "Why me?" question was a start. That had freed up some energy. Perhaps there were other things I could do to use my energy better.

I dimly saw that if I let go of what I had been — all of it, not just the book project — and stopped trying to cling to what I had lost, I could use that energy to promote change. I had many other dreams besides the vision of myself as a children's book illustrator, dreams of who I was and who I would be. All of them were based on the "me" before the stroke. All of them were hard to imagine now. I could turn my face backward, trying to cling to the past and refusing to let go, or...? Holding on to the past is hard work. I knew that letting go was a good idea.

I could begin to show up, pay attention, and discover who I was becoming — right there, in the middle of that rehab hospital — but to find the courage to go as deep as letting go of dreams and moving on required something more than a good idea. To let go at that level required that I find a powerful motivation to live and get on with my life. And that led to the next series of lessons.

PART TWO

# OPENING
# YOUR HEART

# CHAPTER SIX

## *Finding a Reason to Live*

ON THAT DAY OF THE FIRST STROKE, I have to admit I was pretty clueless. It was actually three or four days before someone even said the word *stroke* in my presence, and I was happily hanging out in my fantasy that it would all be over soon. When I got back home and everything was back to normal, I told myself, there would be time enough to call my sons, or so I thought. At this point they were grown men with lives of their own. Fletcher, who lives in Washington State, was thirty-five, and Jacob, who lives an hour north of me, was thirty-three.

Both of them were married, and both had two sons of their own. Patrick and Liam belonged to Fletcher. Alaric and Jonah belonged to Jacob. The little ones were very little at the time. Fletcher's younger son, Liam, was ten months old, and Jacob's younger son, Jonah, was just six weeks old. Bob and I had almost been present when Jonah was born, but Jonah came so fast his mother barely had time to make it to the hospital. Living an hour south, we got there an hour after Jonah.

My sons' lives were full, with wives, children, jobs — with their own concerns. I didn't want to bother them with what I thought was a temporary problem. I've caught quite a bit of good-natured but serious grief from their unhappiness at this decision. And I've had to faithfully promise that if ever I go to the emergency room again and am even minimally conscious, the first call I'll make after calling the ambulance had better be to one of my sons.

When I arrived at the second emergency room and was admitted to the neurological hospital after my first stroke, I was convinced I'd be there only one night for observation and then go home; I thought that whatever this was would quickly resolve itself and I'd get back to the children's book. I watched with some interest and some amusement that first day as my doctor touched me lightly with a pin to see if I had sensation and asked me to move various parts of me. Everything felt odd, but I had sensation and the parts moved, albeit a little awkwardly.

The next morning, after my second stroke, it was clear when I woke up that things were not at all the way I'd imagined they would be. My left arm didn't work. What was that about? My doctor came in early, just as I was waking up, and I said to her, "Doctor, I think I'm worse." She looked at me in shock. I guess she too had assumed I would quickly be back to my life. She reached for her pin and began all the tests again.

In fact, I was indeed worse, considerably worse, but not as bad as I would get. Bob, having seen me safely admitted to the hospital, had driven all the way home to get some clothes. He returned to the area and found a hotel room. He hadn't yet come back to see me. He would shortly learn that I was now in deep trouble.

By the time of my strokes, Bob, the love of my life, was retired from his many professions, but he was still extraordinarily vital. That man was a force of nature — a powerhouse, a storyteller, a philosopher. But even as powerful a force of nature as he was, Bob was in shock to find his much younger wife so gravely ill that she might die. Remember, he knew more than I did. He knew I'd had two brain-stem strokes. I still lacked a framework for what was going on.

Bob came back and sat with me. As the day wore on, it became increasingly evident that I was still getting worse and that things were very serious indeed. By the end of the day, it was obvious even to me that Fletcher and Jacob would have to know, and I asked Bob to call them. It was late when Bob got to the hotel and called. He reached Jacob at home, two hours north of where I was. Jacob must have immediately put down the phone and gotten in his truck and started to drive toward the hospital, because two hours after I'd asked Bob to call, I heard Jacob in the hall.

Jacob is six feet two. He's a contractor. He works out and loves to play rugby. I remember the year Jacob decided to lift weights and strengthen his neck muscles so that when he got into a pile of bodies in a rugby match, he'd keep his neck safe. Now I wonder how he finds shirts that will fit around that neck. It's a good thing he doesn't usually wear ties.

There's nothing Jacob likes better than emerging grinning and battered from a rugby pileup unless it's some other equally forceful guy thing. As I said, he's big. He's also a sweetheart. Jacob can be as tender and kind as you can imagine, with a deep and abiding gentleness of spirit that has been a part of him all his life. The thoughtful tenderness with which he treats his sons is something wonderful to watch. But you don't say no to Jacob. If I'd ever had any doubts about that, the day I took him to be an assistant counselor at a camp and he leapt up on a stubborn horse made it perfectly clear what kind of will he was developing. That horse wasn't interested in having some young-buck stranger on his back. Jacob must have been around fifteen. The horse didn't stand a chance. Jacob rode him through his rearing and his snorting and made it unequivocally clear just who was saying no to whom.

And now there was Jacob in the hall. His booming voice rang out, polite but not a shred of patience in it. "Where's my mom?" he demanded. Then I heard the nurse's voice. I imagined her about five feet two looking up at him. "It's after visiting hours," I heard her reply in a small voice. She might as well have been talking to a brick wall. "Where's my mom?" rang out again. I knew Jacob, and I knew they'd never convince him to leave, so I cried out, in my slurred speech, "Jacob!" And into the intensive-care ward he came.

This neurological intensive-care ward wasn't like the isolation wards I'd seen on TV. This one was a large room with a series of beds around a central nursing station. I think there were six beds. Or maybe eight. I wasn't counting. Each bed had a curtain that went around it, a night table, and a tray table. Jacob came in, found a chair somewhere, and sat by my bed behind the curtain, the curtain so close to the bed that it framed his head and shoulders while his knees touched the mattress. Jacob stayed all night as I moved in and out of consciousness.

At six o'clock in the morning, Jacob's cell phone rang, and I said as clearly as I could, which wasn't very clearly, "If that's your brother, tell him not to come." I still didn't want to bother either of them, and we were a long way from where Fletcher lived. Jacob looked at me with a complex expression somewhere between patience, fear, and exasperation and said, "Too late, Mom. He's already here."

Fletcher is big too, with huge shoulders and a head hard to find hats for. They're both powerful men in so many ways. Put them together in a room, and they take up a lot of space. Fletcher's interests lie more in computers and walking in the woods with his dog than rugby fields. As a child he was inventive and thoughtful, his sweetness immediately evident in his open, sunny smile. As a man, he's also smart and powerful, as well as funny — wonderfully, ironically funny. Ever since he was a little boy, he has had the capacity to say amazingly great lines and see things from an angle other people miss. Fletcher is funny in person, on the phone, and on paper. His emails often reduce me to helpless giggles. Fletcher's humor is so enjoyable because it's infused with the deep kindness and tolerance that inform his life.

When Fletcher was a boy, he had a cat at his father's house named Tasha. Tasha disappeared, and Fletcher looked for her for months. We all told him she was gone for good, but he refused to believe us. One day, sure enough, he found her again and brought her home to live with us. Tasha became the vocal center of our household, moving across the country with us. When we flew to the West Coast and went down to baggage claim to pick her up, her outraged yowls from behind closed doors filled every corner of the baggage claim area. If you're looking for loyalty and commitment, turn to Fletcher.

Fletcher walked in the door, and immediately those two young men formed a tag team. Bob got them a room in the hotel where he was staying, and one or the other of my sons was at my bedside twenty-four hours a day for days as I got worse and worse, until I finally stabilized. If Jacob needed sleep, Fletcher came. If Fletcher needed to eat and take a break, Jacob came. They watched me grow delirious. They watched me lose control of my bladder and bowels, and be put into diapers. Fletcher prevented my wild thrashings one night when I imagined that I could get out of bed. Even in the midst of my wild thrashing, Fletcher's wry humor didn't totally leave him. He calmly said, "Where are you going, Mom?" That brought me up short. Where was I going indeed?

During those early days, I thought I would die. I was, no doubt, close to death. It could have gone either way. I actually didn't mind the idea of dying. Bodies know how to die. There's a point in the process when the body's ready to embrace dying, to experience joy at becoming again a part of what is to be, of pure potential. I wasn't afraid. I could see that it wasn't that hard to let go, and I could easily feel the path toward dying open, as I experienced both the love and gratitude for my life and the opening of possibility for what would come, of life emerging.

The real difficulty came after I stabilized and began to discover how bad off I actually was. I found it hard to believe that I could be so unable to do anything — that when I tried to move nothing happened. That's when I realized I wouldn't die, and if I didn't die, I would have to live with the disability. That's when I thought it would have been so much better if I *had* died. I couldn't imagine how I would cope with my life. This desperation brought me face-to-face with something I needed to learn.

I remember lying in my bed in rehab and making a pact with myself. I was in such despair, thinking I would have been better off dead. I decided that if I didn't get better, I would kill myself. It wouldn't be easy, but I would find a way. My mother had suicided when I was nineteen, and I'd sworn never to do to someone I loved what she had done to my father, my brother, and me. For me to even seriously think about suicide, much less make a pact with myself, showed just how desperate I was.

In this desperate place, in the middle of the night, I couldn't sleep, and I was listening to a tape by Rachel Naomi Remen from her book *My Grandfather's Blessings*. On the tape, Rachel talks about going to medical school with Crohn's disease. I'd read her book several years before, but I'd forgotten this fact. I lay there in the bed, and I thought about this a lot. Crohn's disease is a deeply painful, debilitating disease of the digestive system. Medical school is remarkably demanding, particularly so for a woman in the early days of women moving into medicine. I realized that Rachel had successfully navigated a powerful challenge in the face of a daunting physical difficulty, and I thought that maybe, just maybe, if Rachel could go to medical school with Crohn's disease, there was some possibility that I could face the challenge of my strokes.

Now I had the notion of a possibility of facing this challenge, but the fact that I thought it might be possible still didn't give me any reason to try. One day, lying in my bed in rehab, feeling sorry for myself with my mind wandering, a realization began to dawn on me. Gradually the idea came into focus in my mind. Slowly, tentatively, I wrapped my thoughts around it.

I thought about those two extraordinary young men, those sons of mine. I thought about Bob. I thought about how they had all stood by me when I was so close to death. And finally I got it. Here I was, fifty-five years old, and something really bad had happened to me. And as much as I might wish it otherwise, there was no guarantee that difficulties wouldn't enter the lives of my sons or Bob. I couldn't keep them safe, but maybe I still had something important I could give them.

I realized that it was *my job* as my sons' mother, and Bob's wife, to face what had happened to me and to find a way to deal with it. I owed it to them to try — to set an example that when life is hard, we find a way to deal with it. We don't run away. It was my sacred obligation, and I owed it to them to try. I owed it to Fletcher. I owed it to Jacob. And I owed it to Bob too.

When I realized that, I had a reason to live.

Facing something overwhelmingly hard takes a strong motivation. As long as I was concerned only with myself, I had no reason to get past my personal grief and sense of injustice. But the moment I began to focus on a purpose larger than myself, to realize that life didn't revolve around me, stroke or no stroke, I began to find the strength I would need. In that moment, I saw the situation from a different perspective, and I was able to begin to use myself in a different way.

I had been in my own way. My preoccupation with myself had closed my vision to what was possible. By making a move to get out of my own way, I was beginning to learn how to face what had happened to me. Now I had a reason to live, but I was still pretty negative and there was more I needed to understand.

# CHAPTER SEVEN

## Cultivating Gratitude

MOST OF MY ADULT LIFE, I've espoused the philosophy that there are blessings in everything. I would say to anyone who would listen that it was important to look for the good things in every situation. Then I have two brain-stem strokes in twenty-four hours, and I think, "Yeah, right. There is a blessing in this? I don't think so!" And that point of view persisted for many days. I now had the determination to try to get better, but I was still resolutely negative about what was happening.

I was sitting in my wheelchair, sucking my mental thumb, feeling put upon and sorry for myself, when another realization floated to the front of my mind. What sneaked into my consciousness was this: "Wait a minute. If I've been espousing this philosophy of finding blessings all my adult life, maybe, just maybe, I'd better try practicing what I've been preaching."

And so I decided to try to look for the blessings. Funny thing about intention; as my son Jacob says, "You find what you look for." The minute I began to look for the blessings, I discovered I was surrounded by them. In fact, I'd never experienced so many blessings before in my entire life.

First, there was the incredible blessing of my wonderful husband, Bob, and those two amazing men I'm proud to call my sons. Then there was my brother, Jeff, who flew in from Colorado to see me. I love my brother dearly, and we had spent the last ten years growing closer after many years during which our lives had taken us far away from each other. When Jeff walked into the hospital room, I was speechless with wonder. My brother had jumped on a plane and come to see me!

It may be obvious by now that a big blessing for me was learning that when I could no longer do something for them, the people I loved still loved me and were eager to do something for me. I'd honestly never fully believed this before the strokes; I'd never truly seen the place in other people's hearts I occupied. The understanding was humbling and profoundly sweet.

My father and stepmother in Atlanta who were so concerned were another blessing. My father was too old and ill to travel, but he and my stepmother called me every couple of days. They sent flowers. They talked with Bob and Fletcher and Jacob. They sent cards. Whatever they could do, they did. I don't even know who called them or how they found out. They even offered to try to fly out, but I refused. My father had emphysema and chronic heart failure. Flying was out of the question.

By following his heart and ensuring I was admitted to the neurological intensive-care ward, the doctor in the first emergency room saved my life. If I hadn't already been in the hospital when the second stroke hit, my likelihood of surviving would have been dim indeed. This doctor's medical intuition, which resulted in him insisting that I be admitted despite the neurologist's opinion to the contrary, was certainly another blessing. On New Year's Eve, eight months after my strokes, I walked into the emergency room to tell him so in person. I took his hand, looked him in the eye, and thanked him. He told me, "You made my year." And I said, "And you made mine. You saved my life."

A huge blessing was the opportunity to be in a rehabilitation hospital. Not everyone gets to go to rehab. Hundreds of thousands of people have strokes every year, and the facilities to treat them all don't exist. Physical medicine and rehabilitation is not like any other kind of medicine. It is its own highly developed specialty. The way a trained rehabilitation specialist works with someone with a brain injury or stroke is very different from other kinds of physical therapy. Quickly starting the process of rehabilitation under the guidance of a physical medicine and rehabilitation specialist is critical to an effective recovery.

And I had the privilege of being in the Kaiser Foundation Rehabilitation Center in Vallejo — an extraordinary place. Students come from around the world to study at the rehab center, and with good reason. It is considered one of the top rehab hospitals. I'm a management consultant. I know a good system when I see one. Even with my hard-to-focus eyes, I could gather enough information about how that rehab hospital works to understand just how fortunate I was to be there.

I'm not suggesting to you for a minute that counting my blessings switched me from a state of despair to a stable state of elation, like turning on a lightbulb. Major illnesses are not so simple. Human attitudes are not so simple. I would still spend plenty of time engaged in mental thumb-sucking. What had changed was that I had seen that it was possible to find another way to be with what had happened. Now I was looking beyond self-centered despair from time to time, and reminding myself over and over and over again that blessings are indeed everywhere.

When I came home from rehab, I was still mostly unable to function without using my wheelchair. Although I had a cane and was beginning to take a few steps with it a couple of times a day, I was not walking far. I was wearing the brace that kept my toes from dragging. My gait and balance were precarious, and regular walking was still far beyond my capacities.

There I was on the mountain in a house separated from the garage by that sloped gravel parking area which was uneven and, for me, treacherous. I couldn't walk even a few steps on a straight, smooth surface without a lot of difficulty, much less on a slope. Anything uneven under my feet, and I couldn't compensate enough to be safe. Walk on that gravel? Forget it! It took me months to learn to keep my balance and to strengthen myself enough to be able to get to the garage.

How delighted I was to make it to the garage when I finally did. That was a triumph. But I was far from finished. Still in a brace, I needed to learn to walk up the street I live on. And I mean up the mountain. The street I live on runs at more than a 30 percent slope in some places. I'm not kidding. It's steep and it's narrow, with only enough room for one car at a time. Made of old concrete slabs for most of the length with some asphalt at the bottom, the road is overhung with eucalyptus and redwood trees.

This mountain may be very near San Francisco, but it's still in the woods. It's still rural. Across the main road are state parklands all the way to the ocean. The houses are few and far between. And the mailboxes aren't in front of our houses. The mail carriers have better things to do than drive up and down our steep, narrow roads. If you want the mail and you live on my street, you have to go up that steep, narrow street to the main road. There you will find the mailboxes sitting at attention, all in row.

I had a neighbor who lived halfway up the street, right in the middle of the slope. Getting out of her carport at an angle on that slope was an art. One day, my neighbor saw me attempting to learn to walk up the street. She started coming out of her house every single day and sweeping the concrete surface of the street to eliminate the dirt and small stones that could so easily have upset my precarious balance. She never asked. She never protested. She just swept. That's a blessing, if I ever saw one.

It was June when I came home from rehab; summer was just beginning, and the grasses on the California hills had long since turned to browns and grays. Another neighbor called and then showed up with an entire Thanksgiving turkey dinner — turkey, gravy, stuffing, rolls, mashed potatoes, vegetables, and pie — the whole works. She also brought a big red candle she had been lighting every day since she found out I was injured. That's another blessing.

All the skills and problem-solving abilities I'd learned in my life up to the point of my strokes were there to help me cope. Nothing I ever learned was wasted in the process of recovery. Everything I knew proved to be useful. More blessings.

The blessings were everywhere. I can't begin to count them all. And I've learned something quite useful since I had the strokes. The cultivation of a positive attitude — and gratitude is the fastest means to this I've ever found — changes your body chemistry. No kidding. It lowers blood pressure. It improves the immune system. And I've heard that it may even help to release the hormones in the brain that promote the growth of neural connections.

Bottom line: Gratitude improves my point of view and helps me heal. Quite spectacular medicine! When my attitude improves, my ability to work on my recovery improves. Remember the brain real estate deal? The more and smarter I work, the more likely my brain will be to devote precious resources and start to use itself to make the connections I'm seeking to rebuild. Gratitude is powerful.

Now that I had gratitude and was beginning to appreciate the power of a positive attitude, I began to allow myself to understand the benefits of the next lesson.

# CHAPTER EIGHT

## *Laughter and Lovingkindness*

THERE ARE FUNNY ASPECTS TO EVERYTHING — even a stroke. My son Fletcher knows this. Fletcher looked for the humor from the beginning.

Jacob was close by. After that first week when Bob and Fletcher and Jacob stayed in the hotel near the hospital, Fletcher and Jacob had to get back to their lives. Jacob could continue to commute and bring his big strength and his calm, loving presence to help and comfort me, but Fletcher lived out of state in Seattle. He couldn't easily commute to visit me, so he decided to give me things to comfort and distract me — and to use his humor to cheer me up.

The fingers of my left hand were curled shut. Keeping them curled could cause contractions of the muscles, and I was looking for a way to hold them open. I couldn't easily push them open all day with my right hand, so I needed something with weight. Many items could be used for this, but what Fletcher brought me was a big, bright blue, plastic dog chew bone about eight inches long. I lay in my bed in the hospital with the dog bone holding my fingers open. It looked delightfully weird.

Fletcher has a dog theme going. It's a good thing he has recently gotten a Labrador retriever named Herc who is a fetch maniac. Fletcher relishes having a good dog. When I was in rehab, my eyes wouldn't stay in focus, particularly at a distance, and I couldn't read the clock across the room. My left arm wouldn't work, so I couldn't move it to see the watch on my left wrist. Knowing what time it was helped to orient me, and I missed being able to tell the time, so Fletcher came up with another dog solution. He brought me a soft, floppy stuffed dog. Then he strapped my watch around its neck and called it my "watchdog." That dog and I kept company all through the hospital stay and rehab. I always knew what time it was, and I always felt a little lighter when I checked. I still have that dog sitting on a shelf in the bedroom, and I smile every time I see it.

Hospitals are simultaneously boring and terrifying. It's useful to be able to distract yourself from time to time with something like a book, but I couldn't read because I couldn't keep my eyes in focus. Fletcher and Jacob solved this problem with a little tape player and earphones. With my shaky right hand and a lot of effort, I learned to just manage getting a tape in the tape player and putting the earphones over my head. Fletcher gave me science fiction and fantasy and things to distract me, but he also gave me tapes that were just plain funny.

In rehab, I would wake up, be washed and then helped to dress by the CNA, and finally be put in my wheelchair to eat breakfast and wait to wheel myself to the gym for my first appointment of another day of therapy. Many times I would sit there, put the earphones over my head, and listen to the tapes. Eventually I had the courage to put on the funny tapes. Sometimes I'd be sitting in my wheelchair laughing. The CNA would come in and look at me with wonder.

Bob loved the saying "Angels can fly because they take themselves lightly." I was trying to learn to walk, not fly, but the theory applies to both. When I remembered to laugh, everything got easier. Whatever we find funny can relieve the stress of the situations we find ourselves in. Stress freezes us in place, like a deer, or makes us draw away. Either way, stress doesn't help us cope.

It's okay to laugh in the face of hard times. Laughing doesn't mock what's happening. It doesn't trivialize it. I wasn't laughing at anybody else's misery. I was laughing at the absurdity that life brings, remembering not to weigh myself down. What I was facing was hard enough without relentlessly harping on the hardness all the time. Laughing helped. It unfroze me.

Hospitals can provide great sources of humor. So many things happened to me in rehab that were funny, when I thought about it. The very first night in rehab, the stories began. We had big rooms, much bigger than an ordinary hospital room. In addition to the four beds in each of the corners, there was a wheelchair-accessible shower room into which I was wheeled in a specially designed wheelchair called the *shower chair*, a wheelchair-accessible bathroom, closets along the wall between the shower room and the bathroom, and a big space in the middle for the wheelchairs to move around in. I was in the far right corner as you came in the door, lying by a window that looked out into a small space between buildings with a light that was on all night.

That first night, lying there awake, I was having trouble sleeping, and my roommate diagonally across the room couldn't sleep either. We were pretty far away from each other as hospital rooms go, but not so far that I wasn't sharing in her choice of how to deal with being awake in the middle of the night. Her solution was to watch TV. The TVs come with earphones, but she was unaware of this, and I could easily hear everything.

Two o'clock in the morning, and my roommate was watching reality TV. Seven years ago, reality TV had not yet taken over prime time, and the middle of the night was one of the few times you could find it. There I was, participating from across the room, thankfully without the benefit of being able to see the TV, in my roommate's choice of entertainment: the story of some fool who had locked himself in a glass box, stripped, painted himself with sticky stuff, and gotten bugs to crawl on him. It was beyond weird. And I thought I had problems? Who was this guy? True, I wasn't laughing that first night, but although I wasn't laughing, I realized how wonderfully absurd the situation was even then. Later, when I was lightening up, I remembered the story and delighted in it.

The second day I was in rehab, there was an emergency evacuation drill. I had no idea what was happening when the nurse hurried into my room early in the morning, put me in the wheelchair, and raced me off to a central meeting place with all the rest of the patients. First reality TV, then mad dashes out of my room early in the morning. What silliness was next?

There were many stories, but my all-time favorite story is this: Since the birth of my children with their big heads, from time to time I've had a problem with hemorrhoids. When my hemorrhoids act up, it's usually at night when I'm trying to sleep. They hurt a little and keep me awake. Sleeping was enough of a problem for me in rehab. I didn't need this one, but sure enough, with all the lying down and various other difficulties, the problem returned. It was the middle of the night, and I was uncomfortable with hemorrhoids. I called the nurse. That night there was nothing she could do for me except offer acetaminophen. I couldn't even take aspirin because of the bleed in my brain, but she promised to ask my doctor for some cream, which she did. For days after that, every morning when the day nurse was giving me my various pills, he or she would wave the tube of cream in its plastic bag at me and ask if I needed it. It was a bit embarrassing but worth it to know that although I didn't need it then, it was available if I did.

One night, the pain came back, not severe but annoying. "Aha!" I thought. "Now I can get some relief." With confidence I called the nurse and asked for my cream. This night nurse was a big-shouldered, serious, stern-looking woman. She gravely listened to me and then left, I thought to get the cream. A few minutes later, she marched back into the room. As I eagerly imagined relief, she leaned over me, her face deadpan, and without a clue to how absurd she sounded, solemnly announced, "Sorry, dearie, you can only have that in the daytime."

She really said that! I looked at her in complete astonishment. That part of me really didn't know or care whether or not the sun was shining. The cream was on my chart as a medicine I was authorized to have. It was available over the counter in the drugstore, and if I'd had any of it where I could reach it, even as disabled as I was I probably could have helped myself, but she wouldn't budge. I couldn't believe anybody could take things that literally.

I no longer minded the discomfort at that point because I was thinking how funny this situation was. So I suppose in some sense she helped me, since I fell back asleep smiling. Some years later, I told this story to the head doctor of the rehab hospital as we were standing in a hallway. The two of us laughed so hard we had tears in our eyes.

Finding humor in the midst of my misery, I was lightening up from time to time, but if I was going to help myself, my attitude still required a great deal of adjustment.

## LOVINGKINDNESS

If you've ever wondered if the philosophical system or spiritual practice you work with will do you any good when the proverbial you-know-what hits the fan, wonder no more. In my experience, the answer over and over again is yes. Whenever I speak at the rehab hospital, the people I meet who have a spiritual practice or a philosophical perspective are miles down the rehab road from the ones who don't.

My practice was and is fairly eclectic. I was born into a family of nonpracticing Episcopalians (the only time we ever went to church when I was a child was on Easter), but I was and am a seeker. In my twenties I spent a lot of time in Quaker meetings and still attend when I have the opportunity. Just before I got together with Bob, I came to love Judaism, which nourishes my life, and everything I do is informed by what I've learned and continue to learn from Buddhism. I don't claim to have a deep, committed practice. I don't meditate every single day and I don't go on long retreats, but I do my best to incorporate the teachings of all these paths and make living my daily life my practice.

In the early period after my strokes, I was absorbed in feeling helpless and useless; in other words, I was supremely self-centered. I was convinced that I could do little to change things. I had to get through the first lessons and find some way past my preoccupation with myself before I remembered my practice.

The day I arrived at rehab, I desperately wanted to be able to drink ordinary water. I was still drinking that same gelatinous goo the doctors had started giving me in the hospital. When I asked if I could please drink water, I was introduced to my speech therapist, Kam. I've since come to adore Kam. She has done so much, in her wonderfully warm and expert way, to help me and so many other patients I have known, but when I first got to rehab, I didn't adore her. Kam was the swallowing and cognition police.

The speech therapists in rehab have an inadequate title. In addition to teaching speech, they also monitor swallowing and cognition. They have it tough. PTs and OTs teach you how to do practical things. The work of speech therapists is absolutely critical to regaining speech and cognition, but the effects of their efforts are often not as immediately obvious as those of the PTs and OTs. And speech therapists must also spend a lot of time assessing you and then telling you that you're not ready to do things, like swallowing or making decisions. Perhaps it's better for them that the patients don't know exactly what speech therapists do at first. Sometimes it's hard not to resent them.

Kam wouldn't let me drink regular water. There were things she had to teach me first. I had to learn the chin tuck. What's the chin tuck? In order to slow swallowing, first you drink ice water, not room-temperature water, and you drink only little sips, not big gulps. During all of this, when you swallow you have to put your chin down to the side toward your chest. Tucking your chin closes the airways to your lungs while you learn to swallow correctly. It's a big deal. Failure to swallow correctly puts water in your lungs. Water isn't supposed to be in your lungs. It's supposed to be in your stomach.

I was impatient. I didn't want to wait for my water, but I had to learn to do a chin tuck first. I had to show Kam that I could do it. My irritation grew. Then came the famous day in Kam's office with the checkbook exercise. Kam was supposed to measure my cognition. It was her job. Could I reason correctly? If I couldn't, my family needed to know right away. I might make dangerous decisions. I knew I could reason correctly. I couldn't talk so that most people could understand me. I couldn't see straight, but fortunately I could reason.

Just as with the swallowing, I was going to have to prove to Kam that I was competent. At her table, I was trying to look at a piece of paper with lines on it. Ever try to look at a line when your eyes are out of focus? I was supposed to make entries on this piece of paper with the lines on it, showing that I understood which side of the debit and credit columns the deposits and checks belonged on, placing correct entries on correct lines. Then I was supposed to add all this up with an adding machine. I had an MBA. I had done complex financial spreadsheets. But that cut no ice in rehab. Everybody is equal. Who you were doesn't matter. All that matters is what you can do now. I had to do the checkbook.

Even Kam had a hard time understanding what I was trying to say with my slurred speech and my difficulty breathing, and she is a speech therapist. To top it off, my frustration was triggering laughing and crying, making talking even harder. I sat there struggling to see and struggling to talk, which could easily be interpreted as struggling to think, but wasn't. Finally, with my shaking right hand I put the entries more or less in the appropriate spaces by squinting and closing one eye. Then came the addition. Some adding machines are built in a way that requires you to enter the action before the number doing the action. Some require the symbol be entered after. With my limited understandability, I was trying to ask Kam this overall conceptual question about the logic of the adding machine, and she was trying to figure out if I could take simple cognitive steps. It was bizarre. Fortunately for both of us, Kam's wonderful sense of humor came to the rescue and we got through it.

It's remarkably frustrating not to be able to do the tasks you had taken for granted just a short while ago. I didn't want to be mad and resentful, but I often was. I was trying hard to keep my anger and resentment in check, and I kept casting around for ways that would help me take charge of my healing and make a difference in my own life. That's when I remembered my practice.

All spiritual traditions speak about love and kindness, about treating others well. The method for doing this that I knew best is a Buddhist practice for cultivating lovingkindness. In this practice you first imagine someone you love deeply — maybe your child, maybe your mother, maybe a favorite mentor. You experience the feeling of love for this person as deeply as you can, and then you begin sending it to other people, starting with people you care about and eventually sending it to the people you're having trouble with. The general object is to send positive, loving thoughts to everyone, regardless of whether you're feeling mad and resentful toward them or not.

"Hmm," I thought. "Lovingkindness. What would happen if I started practicing lovingkindness?" There wasn't much I could do lying in my bed or sitting in my wheelchair, but I certainly could do that. Practicing lovingkindness didn't require me to walk or talk or see straight. "Maybe I should try this," I thought. I began an active, intentional practice of treating every person I met in the rehab center with kindness and love, including the night nurse who wouldn't give me the cream, and the night nurse who wanted to be kind and didn't know how and so insisted on waking me up in the middle of the night to plump my pillows. Bless her heart! I wanted to sleep. Bringing lovingkindness to my interactions with Kam was easy. She's the kindest and warmest of women.

There's something remarkable about lovingkindness. It changes the sender more than it changes the receiver, although it changes both. Practicing lovingkindness gave me an active way to participate in what was happening. It opened my heart, and it made me more receptive to being taught what I was in rehab to learn. Resentment is a defense. It closes off opportunity, connection, and effort. Lovingkindness opened me up. Being with my therapists became a heartwarming experience. I looked forward to it. We no longer wasted so much time on my attitude and got right to work with each interaction.

After a while practicing lovingkindness, I began to appreciate how difficult the work of all the therapists is. They see us, the patients, for a few days in our most critical early periods. They help us struggle with the first steps we're taking. They set the tone for all our future rehabilitation, teaching us the tools we'll need to make our recoveries work, keeping us from practices that will make our problems worse. And they rarely get to see us after we have spent the necessary time and energy to claim our new lives. They never see us again unless we go back and visit them. How much courage of the heart does it take to give and give and give every day and rarely see the full results of your efforts?

Many of us in rehab are rather self-preoccupied. I certainly was. After practicing lovingkindness for a while, I realized that I could now do something else. I could take every available opportunity to appreciate my therapists and nurses, my CNAs and doctors, and thank them for what they were helping me discover.

One morning a CNA came to help me put on my shoes. As she was bending over and helping me, the fact that she was in pain became obvious. I asked her what was the matter, and she told me that she had rheumatoid arthritis. For her to do what she was doing was painful for her. Reaching out of my self-preoccupation and simply listening to her story, acknowledging in whatever way I could my appreciation for her effort in helping me, opened my heart. Lovingkindness was now combined with gratitude. Both were helping me heal.

As my heart opened and I became less focused on my personal misery, I was becoming more teachable. Slowly things were changing in my body. Slowly I was learning how to stand on my own, even though at first I didn't know that.

Sometimes Erwin would treat me in the big gym, and sometimes he would treat me in one of the smaller single rooms, just big enough to hold a treatment bed. One day toward the end of my stay at rehab, after having worked with me for a while, Erwin had me sitting on the edge of the bed in the little treatment room. "Stand up without pushing off with your hand," he told me. I waited. What did he mean? Standing up had been a struggle that generally required me to push hard with my right hand and be assisted by someone else. Erwin was a pace away from me, able to reach me if he needed to, but he wasn't looking as if he were going to assist me.

"I can't do it!" I wailed.

"Yes, you can," he said. Erwin always knew exactly where the edge of my abilities was. He never let me hurt myself. He never let me slack off from what I could do for a minute either. But I didn't believe him anyway. "Go ahead and stand up," he said. "Lean forward like I taught you and stand up." I trusted Erwin, but I thought he was surely wrong this time. But he had asked me, so I decided to try. Taking all my courage up to my throat, I did as he requested. I leaned forward over my feet, took a breath, and . . . I stood up! Never one to waste productive time, Erwin said, "Sit down, and do it again." I stood and sat five more times until I was sure I could do it. Even now, thinking about this brings tears to my eyes. I was exultant. I actually stood up on my own!

To come to the place where I was teachable, I first had major limitations to deal with and lessons to learn. All the while I was working on my recovery, my life was going on. I needed to learn to understand this.

# CHAPTER NINE

## *Life Is Happening Now*

PRACTICING LOVINGKINDNESS was teaching me to participate in my own life while I was working on my rehabilitation. Both in rehab and later at home, I was faced with two
major themes: recovery, and living with what I had. Both
were happening at the same time. I couldn't put off my life
while I recovered, and I couldn't put off my recovery while I
lived.

Strokes or other major illnesses or injuries bring limitations. The limitations become unavoidably obvious when
we're suddenly changed by a major injury, but limitations are
actually a part of all our lives. They aren't usually so obvious
as they are immediately poststroke, but we all have them, in
one way or another. Even as much as I've recovered, I still
have them. My left leg remains quite spastic at times, particularly when I'm cold, tired, sick, or emotional, which can
make walking awkward. I can't really run or climb a ladder.
My coordination is unusual and not entirely predictable. Taking unpredictable coordination up a ladder is a dim idea.

I have limitations unrelated to the stroke. I'm five feet
nine. I'll never be six feet two the way Jacob is. I'll never be

able to lift a sheet of plywood as if it were a sheet of paper the way he does. For several reasons, including my age, I can no longer bear children. My body is past that ability. I'll never have the kind of facility with computers that Fletcher has. His mind is organized differently from mine. I'll never be as facile in another language as folks who learned it when they were two. My brain is older and long past the point when accents are easily mastered. We may not think of things like these as "limitations," but limitations simply divide the horizon of our possibilities into directions. The direction of my possibilities doesn't include big physical strength and size and being a computer whiz. Now it also doesn't include living a life unaffected by stroke.

Obviously some limitations feel a lot more limiting than others, but we all have them in one way or another. I've found it useful to remember that limitations, like all the rest of our lives, are constantly changing and re-forming. Even if my physical limitation doesn't seem to move much, the way I work with it and respond to it can change. Recovery is an active, dynamic process of facing limitations, moving through them, and living around them.

Many years ago Bob introduced me to an amazing family therapist, Yetta Bernhard. I swear Yetta had X-ray vision. Sit in front of Yetta, and your deepest secrets were secret no more. Kind and wise, with an ebullient warmth, Yetta taught me a powerful lesson the last time I saw her. She said, "Learn to live around your limitations." She didn't say, "live *with*." She said, "live *around*."

When a tree grows on a rocky mountainside, the tree

roots grow around the rocks, reaching in any direction that works to find the nutrients the tree needs. The tree doesn't say, "Oh, there's a rock. I have to live with that rock and stop growing." The tree grows around the rock. In the long run, it may even become the strongest tree, with the richest life on the mountain. I've seen some amazing root formations down embankments of the mountain I live on.

Living around limitations starts with the question: "How can I do what will bring me joy with what I have?" Simply asking the question is a powerful act. The questions we ask ourselves change the kinds of answers we find, and they change us as well. Being willing to look at how we can live fully with what we have while we are recovering invites life and creativity into all our actions.

The OTs are the masters of the techniques for living around limitations poststroke, or after any other kind of injury or illness. They have the tools and techniques to help to answer our questions and can encourage and support our creativity. Tav was my OT. Bless his heart, he taught me so much in his openhearted, generous way. He responded to my requests for extra work, giving me lots of things to practice after my appointments with him. Some days he would let me stay additional time in the OT room, and he always listened to me when I told him that I wanted to learn how to do something. Together we would work to find a way to accomplish whatever it was.

One day we were talking about the fact that I didn't know how to dress myself. I told him I was ready to learn, so he offered to send Sonya, who is also an OT, to teach me. There are distinct techniques for learning how to dress with one active hand and leg. There's even a one-handed shoe-tying trick. Once my OTs showed me how, I began to dress myself every day. What a morale booster that was! I could do something for myself.

The OT room probably looks odd to an outsider. The tables are filled with toys and Peg-Boards, clay and blocks, and strength-testing machines, and there's even a kitchen. Most people need to know how to make simple meals when they go home from rehab. Working in a kitchen can be dangerous if you're not fully functional. I went to OT five days a week, doing exercises and improving my coordination. One day Tav asked me what I'd like to cook. I was eager to eat. I'd lost a lot of weight in rehab, working so hard and eating hospital food, but I wasn't all that sure about cooking something.

My first major challenge was moving around the kitchen. Walking and standing up were still serious challenges. Tav taught me how to balance myself against the counter and move sideways holding on. He taught me how to move a pot and then move myself. There were a lot of things to learn about pots. Before the stroke, I could always jump if I spilled something. After the stroke, I couldn't afford an accident. I had to learn how to position handles so there was absolutely no chance I could knock the pot over. There was so much about kitchen safety I'd never thought about.

The coping skills and the practice in rehab gave me the confidence that once I was at home, I could find a way to deal with my own kitchen with the limitations I brought home with me. In my own kitchen, the stove is perpendicular to the sink and the refrigerator opens toward the sink, not toward the stove. I had to plan every action in my kitchen to get items from one place to another and keep myself safe. I needed to face and work around my limitations as they affected my actions in the kitchen so I could prepare simple meals. If I wanted to eat, I needed to learn.

Rita, the friend I mentioned earlier who didn't talk for a year and a half, has a great deal to teach on the subject of living around limitations. When she and I talk with patients together, her strength and good humor fill the room. Her courage and perseverance inspire me and everyone she meets. Before her strokes thirteen years ago, Rita was an acupuncturist, specializing in both acupuncture and acutonics. Acutonics involves holding vibrating tuning forks over acupuncture points to stimulate them. The effect is similar to and different from acupuncture, but without the needles, and is very effective.

Rita was traveling in Tibet up on a mountain when her strokes happened. Thirteen years ago not as much was known about stroke as we know now, although Rita received immediate and effective treatment. In addition to her loss of speech, her right side, arm, and leg were paralyzed, her swallowing reflex was impaired, and Rita was using a wheelchair. Rita is right-side dominant. That means she lost the use of the hand she used most.

No more acupuncture or many other things for Rita, for a while. The doctors told her she would maybe learn to walk with a quad cane someday, if she worked really hard, and she would always need to wear a brace. The doctors didn't know Rita very well. Rita began to try to walk six weeks after her stroke. In order to keep her balance, she'd get behind and push the wheelchair in front of her like a walker. She took the brace off as soon as she could and began to teach her right foot to hold its position. It took five years for Rita to develop a reasonably normal gait. She traded the quad cane for a single-point cane within two months of starting to walk. Rita still has some gait problems. Hers are a little bit more obvious than mine, but she hasn't worn a brace for years, and she no longer uses any kind of cane.

Do Rita's ongoing limitations stop her from doing what she likes? No. Rita likes to hike. The other day she called me and told me she wanted to see the wildflowers and the waterfall on the back of the mountain. I said, "Sure." I like to hike too. I didn't know what I was getting into. This hike turned out to be about five miles over uneven terrain. I use a walking stick on uneven terrain. Rita doesn't, and she easily out-hiked me even while stopping to take pictures of the flowers.

The waterfall was great. Rita brought a picnic, and we sat watching and listening to the movement of the water. At the falls, we met some lovely folks, one of whom, a man in his eighties with two new knees, has been leading hiking excursions for years. Rita hooked up with them and recently went with a group on a nine-and-a-half-mile downhill hike (downhill is much harder poststroke than up) along the coast at Point Reyes. I'm now challenged to try longer hikes so I can keep up with her.

Since her strokes, Rita has focused professionally on

acutonics. While she has taught herself to be highly competent in performing acupuncture with her left hand, she prefers
acutonics because she has found it to be more effective. I'd
never heard of acutonics before I met Rita, but she has done
it on me and it's powerful indeed.

Rita treats people and animals one-handed with her non-
dominant hand. Everyone who gets a treatment loves it. One
of Rita's patients, a highly respected healer, had low-back pain
and sciatica. After two acutonics treatments, both the low-
back pain and the sciatica disappeared. And Rita tells me that
the humans are not the only ones who love the work. Animals understand and respond to it immediately. She treated a
dog with a broken leg who, after the leg healed, had difficulty
putting his paw in the correct position in order to be able to
walk. The vet wanted to perform an operation that would fix
the paw in place, no longer permitting flexibility in the ankle.
A series of acutonics treatments have allowed the dog to both
position the paw correctly and retain flexibility.

But my favorite story of Rita living around her limitations
is this: Rita is a great cook. Maybe I like this story so much
because I get to savor the results of it, when I'm lucky. Once
when we were having a snack before going to speak one
night, Rita brought me some soup that was so good it was all
I could do to refrain from sticking my tongue in the thermos
and licking out the last little bits. Rita likes to cook, and as
I've mentioned she has the use of her one nondominant hand.
Back to the OTs. OTs know all about adaptive equipment for
the kitchen and everywhere else. There are special tools for
working in the kitchen with one hand. There are rocking

knives, cutting boards with spokes in them to hold the object being cut, electric chopping devices — many tools. If you want to learn how to maximize your ability to get on with your life postinjury, be sure to talk to an OT.

Do you imagine that cooking for herself is enough for Rita? If you do, you don't know Rita. Rita is gregarious, generous, and a member of several circles of friends and groups. Rita delights in cooking meals for twenty-five people for four-day workshops. Twenty-five people, one-handed, with her non-dominant hand! Is that living around her limitations, or what?

My friend Carol Howard-Wooten is another example of living around limitations. Carol had a stroke more than twenty years ago, when she was thirty-eight. At the time of her stroke, Carol had just finished graduate school and her practicum for licensure as a marriage and family therapist. After her stroke, her life was shattered, or so she thought at first. As Carol struggled with her physical therapy, rebuilding her ability to walk and move her left hand, she began to think about what she could do with her experience. Carol realized that she now had a unique perspective on life: She was both trained as a therapist and trained by life in the difficulties of stroke recovery.

Carol's response to this realization was to combine the two. For years now, Carol has run groups for stroke survivors. She works with people to help them emotionally deal with what has happened to them. And now Carol has started a nonprofit to continue and expand the work. Carol was the one who arranged for and taught the storytelling class that I took. In her class, I discovered I like telling stories. Now I can stand up in front of a group of people and talk about my experience. Carol allowed me to see that the stroke had cured my stage fright, and gave me the skills to use my experience in a new way. Before my strokes, I didn't feel comfortable in front of an audience. I wondered if I looked okay and if what I said made any sense. I was really worried I would make a mistake and embarrass myself. Now, having shown up in rehab so spastic I couldn't walk, and having been unable to keep from drooling on Julia, how I looked no longer seemed to matter much. If I'd survived that, I knew I could survive standing up and talking to a group of people. Carol's response to her limitations has been to use them to empower other people to grow and live around their own.

As I said, my limitations continue to affect my life. Most people don't see them. But they really are there. It's nearly impossible for me to safely go down a flight of stairs without a handrail if I'm cold and my left leg becomes more spastic. There are places on my property I won't risk walking alone. But these days I've come to understand something important. Life contains more possibilities than I can ever begin to take advantage of. Even if I recovered every bit of the coordination and strength I had the day before the stroke, I couldn't begin to take in all that life has to offer. Every day I have a choice. I can choose to focus on my limitations and thus stay limited, or I can choose life. I choose life.

I know that now. I didn't know it in the early stages of my recovery. While I was in the midst of my recovery and still facing the lessons I needed to learn in order to work through the challenges of my recovery, I wasn't ready to see

the bigger picture. I was struggling with the day-to-day challenges of learning to work with my new limitations, right
here, right now.

Buddhist practice has a lot to say about learning how to
stay present, right here, right now. Jack Kornfield, a well-
known Buddhist teacher, likes to say, "As often as we might
want it to be different, this is it, this moment. This is our life."

When I came home from rehab, I wished a lot of things
were different. I wished my bed weren't in the middle of the
living room to make it possible for me to get into the wheelchair from it. I wished the chairs weren't so low, so I could get
in and out of them without being scared when I wanted to sit
somewhere other than the wheelchair. I wished I could walk
to the garage. I wished brushing my teeth wasn't an ordeal. I
wished I had two working hands that would allow me to floss
my teeth. The list of my wishes was endless.

But I couldn't do those things when I got home, and I
could do even fewer things at the beginning when I was still
in rehab. What mattered was to find the things I could do.
And that required learning the next lessons.

PART THREE

# STARTING FROM WHERE YOU ARE

# CHAPTER TEN

## *Who Can You Be Now?*

BEFORE MY STROKES, I had a habit of doing a lot of things at once. Many of us like to call this multitasking, and we think it makes us very efficient. What might really be efficient is the ability to switch rapidly from paying complete and patient attention from one thing to another, but in my life that was rarely what multitasking meant. Multitasking for me usually meant not paying attention to where I was.

I've long worn many hats, as the metaphor goes. I was a businesswoman, an artist, a mother, a wife, a grandmother, a friend, an advisor, a spiritual seeker, a traveler, a singer, and, and, and. . . . Even within those categories, I was always up to something new. If I loved painting in chalk pastels, I wouldn't settle there; I would try watercolor or mixed media. I'm all in favor of creativity, of trying new things and opening possibilities. The trouble is that in my impatience and hurry I was often someplace else when I was supposed to be *somewhere*. When I was talking with a friend, I might also be planning dinner while I was half listening. When I was spending time with a grandchild, I might be preoccupied with a work problem. The word *preoccupied* is telling when you think about it; you are *pre*-occupied; you are occupied with something else even *before* you start.

When I didn't like what was going on, I'd spin a story about how it would be different someday, when I got around to fixing or changing it, and I'd hang out in the story. That way I didn't have to deal directly with what was actually present. I could avoid looking at things too closely.

The stroke made it clear that the strategy of trying to be somewhere else was no longer going to work very well. The illusions created by my stories were pretty hard to maintain sitting in a wheelchair. Now that my usual stories were unavailable to me, essentially missing, I felt lost and empty. That brought me face-to-face with the next lesson.

Every day of my life I'd told myself stories: stories of who I would be that day, stories of what my life would look like, stories of who would love me and who wouldn't, stories of how competent I would be that day (or how incompetent, if I was feeling down). Before I got out of bed in the morning, my mind had a story about how I would start my day, what I would wear, what I would have for breakfast, how I would get where I was going that day, how I could help others when I got there, what they were likely to think of my efforts — many stories. My head had been filled with stories.

Suddenly those stories didn't work anymore. I couldn't tell myself the usual morning story about how I was going to get up and go to work, either on the book or with a client in my consulting business. I couldn't get out of bed by myself, much less go to my closet. I couldn't successfully negotiate the decision to wear anything more than pull-on pants and a loose pullover shirt. I no longer knew how to close a button. I'd learned how to do that with two hands, not one. Tav sent Sonya to teach me how to dress myself but only in loose-fitting clothes without zippers or buttons.

I have a dear friend, Betty Joan, who is a doctor of physical and rehabilitative medicine, a specialty called *physiatry*, which focuses on rehabilitation. The doctors at the rehab center were physiatrists. Betty Joan and I had met at a conference in Mexico we'd attended several years earlier with our husbands. Bob, who knew Betty Joan before I did, sat us down at a table together in the open-air dining room and said to the two of us, "You have to know each other." As usual, he was right. We're a lot alike and have had many heart-to-heart conversations since that day in Mexico.

Early on, Betty Joan came to visit me in the rehab hospital. She reviewed my records, talked to the doctors, and sat in a chair next to my bed. "Hooray," I thought. "Betty Joan is my dear friend. We don't hide things from each other. Now I have someone who will really tell me the truth about how much I will recover." So I asked her point-blank, "How much will I get back?"

I was looking for a story to tell myself about how I would be. I wanted something to hold on to. Betty Joan looked me straight in the eye and told me what the other doctors knew but hadn't directly said. She said to me, "Nobody knows. It depends on the nature of your body and your brain injury and you. And nobody knows." I didn't want to hear that. I was frustrated. I wanted a story to tell myself.

I didn't realize at first that Betty Joan had given me a

tremendous gift. She had given me the gift of no story. I didn't understand it that day, but not having a story became a powerful tool in my recovery. Being without a story allowed me to be open to not knowing, to discovering.

But, right then, being without a story felt scary. Without a story about who I would be that day, who was I anyway? Without a story, I was left with looking at where I was. And I didn't like where I was.

If I weren't the nice comfortable stories, what was left? If I weren't the successful beginning illustrator, the thoughtful business consultant, the agile mountain walker, the good cook, the decent housekeeper, the ticketless (or nearly) car driver, what was there?

If the doctors couldn't know and therefore didn't tell me what my future would look like, what story could I make up?

Being without a story made me feel naked, unprotected. But being without a story was going to force me to look seriously at something that both my friend Stanley Keleman and Buddhism had been saying for years. Both Stanley Keleman and Buddhism had taught me that I was not a fixed self to be preserved or lost. Not only was my body re-forming constantly, but also the "I" inside me was truly a process, something constantly changing. All my stories talked about a more or less fixed person, someone measurable, someone you could quantify and put in a category. But were those categories really me?

The categories I'd happily put myself into suddenly disappeared. If I could lose all my stories in the moments it took my brain to bleed and suddenly wind up in some other category and still be "me," who was I?

It had been easy to intellectualize the ideas of impermanence that I'd been taught and to think I understood them when I hadn't lost so much all at once. A little loss or gain here and there, fitted into the chinks in my well-constructed story of myself, was easy to accommodate. This much change was not.

I was, quite frankly, terrified. I cast around for some way to deal with the terror. How could I get away from the fear? Buddhist and Quaker practice had taught me that although I couldn't get away from the fear, there was something that might help me deal with it. I wasn't keen on this approach or any other just then. I didn't want to look at the fear. I wanted to escape from it, but I had no choice. There was nowhere to go.

I'd been learning to sit with emotions, even fear, when I meditated. I knew from trying this practice that feelings are another thing that's not permanent. Emotions come and go. As the emotions come and go, it's sometimes possible to sense something else, to sense the ineffable — something bigger than the emotions, something deeper, vaster, calmer. The practice had taught me also that somehow "I" was connected to something larger than myself. That knowledge had helped me face dying. Now that knowledge was going to help me face the fear of living without my stories.

I didn't want to sit with fear. I didn't want to experience it, but I thought if I could practice being with the fear, maybe I could find the courage to bear the fear and not try either to push it away or to hold on to it. And if I could do that, perhaps the fear would eventually pass, like the other emotions I'd worked with while meditating. I knew the fear wouldn't disappear forever, but it could pass. That was the theory. Could I put it into practice?

The middle of the night was the lowest point of the day for me. I remember the bed in my room in rehab. I remember being unable to move in that bed, trying to reach for the nurse's call button when it was out of my grasp, hanging there on the television that swung on an arm over the bed. Sometimes when the nurses made the bed, they'd forget and push the television out of reach. I remember wanting things on my tray table but being unable to get to the tray table unless the nurse came and put it right beside me.

Darkness wrapped around me while I lay in that bed in the middle of the night. I couldn't see the clock. Thankful for the soft toy dog with the watch around its neck, I held it against my chest. In that bed in the middle of the night: "Wake up, wake up!" — time to be catheterized. "Wake up, wake up!" — time to have my blood pressure checked. The blood pressure machine on its stand rolling around that four-person room from bed to bed. "Your turn next."

I remember lying awake, alone. It was harder than trying to walk. It was harder than sitting in the dining room and feeling foolish eating in front of other people with all my limitations. The middle of the night was when the fear was the most difficult to bear because there was nothing to distract me from it — no classes, no food trays, no phone calls. That's when the lack of stories really showed up. Sometimes I could occupy myself with tape recordings, which were full of other people's stories, welcome words, contact. But sometimes I couldn't.

One night when I was awake and filled with fear, I decided to try to put into practice what I'd been taught. I lay in my bed, experiencing my breathing as I'd been instructed to do, meditating and just noticing the fear, feeling for the spaciousness in which the fear floated. After a while of noticing, the fear moved a tiny bit, and I fell asleep. I tried this another night, and another, and eventually I began to realize that I could be with the fear and the fear would indeed move on. I could see a way to show up in the midst of the fear and work with it. I was still scared, but I was no longer desperately seeking to get away from the fear.

The practice of being with the fear changed my relationship to it. Slowly, I became able to find a little bit of spaciousness around the fear even when I wasn't meditating. Slowly I found a way to be with the fear and not let it drive me away from being able to really look at what was true about my life now.

Trying to avoid the fear was keeping me from looking hard at anything else. If I could be with the fear of being storyless, I could start to look at what being storyless really meant. I could begin to honestly look at where I was. So one day when I was feeling brave, I took a peek past the fear. When I looked past the fear, what immediately came up was grief. A major source of the fear had been my unwillingness to confront all the losses.

The truth was, I'd lost a lot. I couldn't push that aside. I couldn't pretend it hadn't happened or distract myself from dealing with it. I needed to acknowledge and then grieve the losses before I could do anything else. My stories were gone. The book was gone. My ability to travel with Bob was gone. My ability to hold my new grandchildren was gone. So much was gone.

Loss is loss. The path to the other side of loss is through grief. There is no going around it. Grief repressed, or distracted by stories, becomes a dangerous psychic force, turning into depression, erupting in anger and frustration at something only dimly related to the original cause, draining energy. I needed my energy. I would have to grieve. Grief was in my way. Transformation wasn't possible without acknowledging the grief and dealing with it.

I wept.

Acknowledging the grief — and weeping — wasn't easy, and it wasn't fun. But it eased my heart and allowed me to begin to open my eyes to whatever the truth of what happened might be, just as it was — no pretending. Grieving brought with it the capacity to treat the situation I was in with some compassion. It allowed me to begin to be able to look really closely at what exactly I had and didn't have in the way of function. What could I do? What couldn't I do?

When I solved problems in the real estate business — for example, when I had to repair a roof — I didn't make up a story about it. I really looked at the situation. In the case of a roof, I examined all the spots that were breaking down and worked with the roofer to create a thorough plan to fix them. I wasn't a roof, but the theory was the same. If I wanted to change something, I was going to have to start from right where I was — not from someplace I imagined myself to be.

I would have to acknowledge the loss, allow myself to feel the grief, and begin with what I had. If I couldn't bend my knee, finding a way to learn how to bend my knee was where I had to start. If I couldn't move my fingers or needed a bib to catch the food I spilled with my shaky right hand, that's where I was. In some ways it was as simple as that. What is, is.

But working with what was actually happening would require me to see it clearly. Seeing it clearly required cultivating the skill of paying attention. I could start the process of dealing with the grief and I could decide to look as clearly as I could at my situation, but I still needed to learn to focus my attention.

# CHAPTER ELEVEN

## *Paying Attention*

PAYING ATTENTION HELPS. That seems self-evident, but actually it's not, or it wasn't for me. Throughout my recovery, I was to learn this lesson in ways I'd never imagined. Finding a path to recovery, along with the ongoing discipline of living with my limitations, has given me an extraordinary opportunity to witness and discover the powerful benefits of simply paying attention.

I was now prepared to start from where I was — to be able to see what was true — so I asked myself, "How can I help myself pay attention?" I realized I had some tools I could use that came from my experience. I'd been a watercolor painter. Watercolor painting requires close attention. The medium is fickle, sensitive, and very difficult to correct if you make a mistake. I'd practiced paying attention when I painted — being still and looking closely. What I'd learned while painting was a tool I could use. When I thought about it, I remembered what it was like to be still and focused and to look closely at the brush. I could look at my body the same way. I could visualize my body as if it were a brush moving in a painting that I was creating.

That was one tool, and I had another. Meditation teachers have a lot to say about paying attention. In meditation I'd learned about something called *mindfulness*. Mindfulness is the skill of simply looking at what's happening without trying to judge it or measure it, without grasping it or pushing it away — not holding on to something and not running away from it — not trying to judge myself as good, bad, right, wrong, but simply paying attention to what's happening. This paying attention is anchored in the breath. Notice the breathing — in, out — and notice what arises and passes away in the midst of the breathing. Meditation had helped me deal with the fear. Now mindfulness practice could help me pay attention.

Breathe, notice, notice, notice, breathe, over and over again. It's harder than it looks. The mind wanders and is easily led off in some direction or another. I needed to focus, to really allow myself to be absorbed in what I was experiencing, not what I interpreted about what I was experiencing, not what I dearly wished I was experiencing or really didn't want to be experiencing, simply noticing what was.

The Buddhist teacher Frank Ostaseski, who founded the Zen Hospice in San Francisco, has a teaching I particularly like. He says, "Welcome everything. Push away nothing." That's paying attention.

I began to practice paying attention, trying to simply be where I was, saying to myself over and over again, "Welcome everything. Push away nothing." Difficult things would happen. I'd be put in the shower chair to be given a shower, I'd be wheeled into the shower room, and someone would wash me. I liked having a shower. I didn't like not being able to give myself one; I didn't like having someone else wash me. "Welcome everything. Push away nothing." The situation was just as it was. I could notice the pleasant warm water, the struggle to help to wash my hair one-handed, my feelings about it, the way my arm moved — all of it. Pay attention. Notice.

When we push something away, when we avert our attention from it, we don't allow ourselves to learn. Once while walking on the mountain before my strokes, I saw a rock and thought, "Oh, a boring gray rock," and turned aside. As I pulled my eyes away from it, I realized I was pushing it away, not taking it in, so I looked back and began to gaze at the rock, paying attention. When I began to pay attention, to be with the rock just as it was, I saw that the rock was not simply gray; in truth, it was a symphony of subtle colors. How beautiful it was. Welcoming it, not pushing it away, I saw the rock's wonderful visual harmony.

The immediate reaction to an injury from stroke may be to push away the part of ourselves that's injured and not want to be with it. When we do this, there's no information available for us to work with. We only see the gray, never noticing all that might really be there.

I began to do my best to notice everything, focusing carefully on whatever really was happening and how I reacted to it, just as it was, without making it right or wrong, without grasping or denying it. In this way I discovered how to work with and encourage my brain's reconnection with my body.

There are many types of physical therapy, some directed at

orthopedic problems such as hip replacements, and others for the specific constraints imposed by brain injuries. One of the types of therapy practiced at the rehab hospital is PNF, short for *proprioceptive neuromuscular facilitation*. I've been told that, among other things, PNF stimulates the ancient reflexes embedded in the brain and spinal cord. If the brain doesn't remember the way to a particular action, perhaps bypassing the brain and going directly to the spinal cord will help.

One night, hours after Erwin had been working with me, moving my left leg over and over again in many different directions and working with my foot, something happened. I was lying in my bed, just waking up. All of a sudden, out of what seemed like nowhere, my left ankle, which had done nothing at all since the stroke, jumped — a simple reflex jump. Instantly I woke fully up and paid very close attention. I could hear my brain joyously exclaim, "Ankle? ... Ankle!!! ... I remember you!!!" I couldn't move my ankle voluntarily that day, but I could remember the feeling. I could remember the recognition of my brain, and I could focus and encourage it. I'd been paying attention.

I started paying attention for any sign of connection between my brain and my ankle, no matter how minute. I kept nourishing that feeling of momentary connection, noticing how it felt to nourish it, noticing how my brain responded. Several days later, the reflex jump happened again. I paid even more attention. And then, very gradually, I began to find my way back to my ankle. I began to be able to move it voluntarily. The movement was small, weak, and not well coordinated at first, but it was a beginning.

I didn't know then what I know now. Now physiatrists and neurologists have learned that even just thinking about moving a limb begins to create new neural pathways. Sitting and imagining walking, with focused attention, makes a difference in our ability to walk. Rehearsing in your mind how you will play a piece of music makes a difference in how you play it. The more I focused my attention on what I was trying to do, encouraging the ways my brain could reconnect with the rest of me, the more likely it became that something would happen. Paying attention trains the brain and asks it to devote resources to support effort. Attention is powerful. Attention contains within it the potential for action.

When the fingers of my left hand began to move again, the beginning motions were tiny. My left thumb began to twitch, just fractionally, when I thought about it. Nothing else in my hand moved, but there was that little twitch. Again I focused, watched, and followed each tiny movement and encouraged it; I paid attention. And as I paid attention, very, very gradually the movements got bigger. Very, very gradually the control become more voluntary, and then very, very gradually the first finger joined the thumb. The movements of my fingers unfolded from the center outward, with the pinky being the last to move. This unfolding happened over many months — not all at once. The more I paid attention, the more the process of unfolding continued.

I continued to practice mindfulness sitting in my room in rehab. I wasn't always meditating; I was simply being still and noticing what was happening with me. Were my fingers moving? Could I find my toes? What did it feel like to have a limb that I could see and feel but couldn't voluntarily move? What did it feel like when I uncurled the fingers of my left hand and stretched them with my other hand? Notice. Pay attention. The more I paid attention, the more I called my brain into action.

One of the mindfulness practices in Buddhism is walking meditation. In short retreats I'd attended, a common practice to help me learn to stay present in the moment was to spend time silently walking while concentrating on the walking itself, to notice when my feet moved, how they touched the ground, when each leg swung forward. This wasn't designed to be an intellectual evaluation of the theory of walking. This exercise was designed to teach me to notice what my body was doing and to be fully present in the action of walking.

Ordinarily, outside of a retreat, I would have been running the usual stories through my brain. I would be walking and thinking about what I'd said to somebody the day before, replaying it in my mind, editing all the while, saving the good parts, excising the bad parts. Or I would be planning a trip for me and Bob, seeing myself in an airplane with him. Or perhaps thinking about the grocery list, or the color I was painting bears, or the client who needed an answer — everything and anything but what I was actually doing, which was walking. Ordinarily my attention would have been nowhere close to where I was. I could take an entire walk on a path on the mountain for an hour or more, and not see anything except the images created by the conversation in my head. No birds, no lizards, no trees, no grasshoppers, no blue sky — nothing.

Walking meditation had given me another approach to walking. I decided to try it in the rehab gym. What exactly was my foot doing when I tried to move my left leg? What action was my knee taking? What did the movement of my left hip feel like? Attention. Attention. Attention. "Wow!" I thought. "This is really useful." I found that the more I paid attention, the more I could manage some kind of a walking gait. It wasn't smooth. It wasn't coordinated, but I was moving holding on to those parallel bars. I asked Erwin if I could stay later in the gym and try some more, and he agreed. I kept at it. "Pay attention. Watch the foot in particular," I thought.

Then I came home. Rehabilitation at home provided non-stop opportunities for paying attention. I needed to learn how to go up and down the curved staircase if I wanted to take a shower. My bed was upstairs. The upstairs bathroom had a tub shower. There was no way I could use that. I couldn't get in and out of a bathtub if my life depended on it.

I had to get downstairs to the walk-in shower. The little house I live in was built many years ago as two small apartments that weren't connected inside. When Bob had the house remodeled, his friend Roger created a small round tower attached to the back corner of the structure to contain a staircase that curves around, made of wooden steps. This staircase was not built with a disabled person in mind. Walking up and down it with a stiff and unresponsive left side required every bit of attention I could bring.

Everything required a great deal of attention. Walking on the gravel between the house and garage required me to know at any given moment just how my foot was responding to the uneven surface so I wouldn't lose my balance. Being able to pay attention was proving to be a crucial skill.

And it still is. Today I can walk, much of the time, in a way that makes it very hard for anyone except someone who knows stroke really well to detect I ever had one. Sometimes you can detect a hitch in my gait, but, like the man who once said to me, "Oh, I have a sore foot too," most people can't identify what caused it. Have I stopped paying attention? No. Today I can walk so well precisely because I continue to pay attention, all the time, to what my left foot is doing.

When a person who is unaffected by brain injury walks, the foot comes down heel first and then rolls through a step. As that person prepares for the next step, the toes of the foot automatically swing up and clear the floor. The toes on my left foot do that sometimes. But sometimes they don't. To walk easily requires that a part of my mind constantly pay attention to the position of the toes on my left foot and be prepared to consciously tell them to swing up when it doesn't happen automatically. That's my reality. Paying attention allows me to take five-mile hikes and walk along busy streets.

Now that I was paying attention, and my recovery was unfolding, what else did I need to learn?

# CHAPTER TWELVE

## *The Art of the Small Goal*

A COMMON RESPONSE TO A STROKE or other brain injury is the loss of some degree of impulse control. I definitely experienced this particular problem. I wanted to do everything right away. No waiting. No interim steps. I had a tendency to go from zero to one hundred without a pause even before my strokes. My brain injury exacerbated this tendency.

The problem with this approach is that it doesn't work. I could no longer go from zero to one hundred. I couldn't go from being in a wheelchair to taking long walks. It seems self-evident now. But when I was in the middle of it, it didn't seem self-evident at all.

I was trying to pay attention to where I was, but I very much wanted to blow past the fear I was learning how to be with and reassure myself that everything was okay by being able to do things.

Not so fast. Recovery doesn't work that way.

Recovery entails mastering the art of the small goal. Recovery requires doing what you can now and not knowing what you can do later — working without assurance that you will achieve the big goal but working anyway. I was a big-picture person. I could see the steps in a process that led to a specific result. That's a useful strategy for fixing roofs. It's not such a useful strategy for recovery. Now I know that it's not always the most useful strategy for life either.

I had a lot to learn about how to stay present as I moved through the process of recovery. I had a lot to learn about the power of not knowing the answers before I asked the questions. Before my strokes, I would ask a question and unconsciously filter the response for the answer I was seeking. I wasn't so good at asking open-ended questions. I typically had an agenda, usually without knowing it was there. "Hidden agendas," Bob called them.

A hidden agenda could be something as simple as having decided the result I intended to get before I began, or as complex as trying to make other people wrong no matter what they said. Let's say I have some railings to paint. Knowing that the result I want is a completely painted railing before I start is a practical agenda — clear, not hidden. But thinking I know what you'll say about something before I even listen to your response is not; that's a hidden agenda. For example, when I listened to the doctor in the first emergency room, I only heard the part of what he said that I wanted and expected to hear. I didn't pay attention to the rest.

Having a closed mind — a predetermined, hidden agenda about what constituted successful walking — was not going to help me find a way to walk. If I decided that my foot had to be in a particular position to be "right," I set myself up for failure. All I'd see about my walking was a judgment that I didn't get it right because my foot wasn't where

I'd decided it had to be. That kind of agenda wouldn't allow me to discover that the first thing I had to do wasn't really about my foot. The first thing I had to do was find a way to balance on my left leg as I shifted my weight from one leg to another.

Focusing on small goals, one at a time, not on some pre-determined outcome, opens the process up to discovery. Small goals met lead to larger results. I was learning to balance my weight on my left leg. I was learning, through the bridging exercise, to hold my trunk strong. Once I'd gained some skill with those goals, other goals arose. I began to regain control of bending my knee, of some movement in my left calf, of a forward motion with my left hip. All small goals.

My toes still wouldn't flip up, but I'd been fitted for a brace, which was a plastic sheath running up the back of my calf and cradling my foot, held on by Velcro straps around the front. Control over the position of my foot came many months later when I learned to walk without the brace. Between my initial steps and walking without a brace stretched a long process of many small achievements. When I left the rehab hospital, I was very unsteady. I could walk only a few steps at a time. I had no way of knowing whether I would ever achieve walking without a brace when I started. I had to work on one step at a time, discovering each day how much I might be able to walk.

Since most of my recovery would take place after I left rehab, dealing with my impulse-control problems, accepting the reality of small goals, and slowing down were critically important factors. Back to the mats. I had been racing through my sets of bridging. If I could do two or three sets of ten, maybe I could do six or seven sets. I can still hear the voice of the lovely Austrian woman directing the mats class. "Slowly, Alison. Slowly," she'd say. The object wasn't to race ahead to seventy repetitions. The object was to do one at a time, very well.

One at a time, very well. That's the key — focusing on each goal, each day, showing up and doing the very best I could with what I was able to do. That willingness — to let go of the future and work with what I had — made a very big difference. It was absolutely necessary that I refuse to let my impulse-control problems rule me and that I learn to work with what I had. I was going home. When I got home, goal setting was my responsibility. Nobody else would do it for me.

On the wall in my kitchen is a wire shelf with cookbooks on it. My favorite cookbook is the classic *The Joy of Cooking*. I particularly like this book because it weighs in on almost every subject. Because it covers so much material, the book itself weighs a lot. It's big. To put a cookbook away on that funny wire shelf requires two hands, one to pick up the book and one to push the other books away to make a space. There's no way to put the cookbook back with just one hand. *The Joy of Cooking* sits on the extreme left side of the shelf. If I wanted to use it and put it away again, I was going to have to learn to use both hands and lift the book with my left.

By the time I came home, I'd gained some movement in my left arm and hand but very little strength and coordination. There was no way I could even pick *The Joy of Cooking* up in my left hand, much less raise it to the shelf level and put it away while I used my right hand to move the other books away. What could I do? What I'd begun to be able to do is to lift very light things with my left hand and arm and put them up a short distance.

I had to figure out how to get from where I was to the possibility of lifting the heavy cookbook. How I decided to work was to devise a series of small goals to strengthen my left arm and hand. I had a general goal of being able to put *The Joy of Cooking* back on the shelf. I didn't know if I could achieve it, but I knew I could lift something light, so I started there.

I lifted a very small can to a shelf in the cabinet, over and over again, day in and day out, until I mastered the movement and was comfortable with it. Then I tried to do the same thing with a slightly larger can. Again I raised it to the shelf and took it down repeatedly. Then I used a much larger can, and then an even larger can. Slowly my ability to raise my left arm while holding something improved. Slowly I was able to lift heavier cans. Once I'd accomplished that, I tried lifting the heavy cookbook a short distance. I could pick it up. I was elated. Again I practiced the repetition of this simple act until I was ready to try for the next goal of being able to lift the cookbook higher up. Finally, one day I was able to reach the bigger goal. I actually put *The Joy of Cooking* away on its shelf. I was thrilled. I think about that day every time I use this well-worn cookbook.

Throughout the process, while I hoped that someday I would have enough use of my arm and hand to put the cookbook away with it, I couldn't know if I would ever succeed. I couldn't know if I would successfully make it past any of the levels of cans I was using. Not knowing, I tried anyway. I focused on the immediate smaller goal and discovered what I could do in each part of the process.

There's magic in this. Being willing to hang out in the big "don't know" and work anyway creates possibilities. Being willing to do the very best I could with what I had in front of me, without trying to control or predict the outcome, opened the door to discovery. The truth is my imagination isn't big enough to forecast all the amazing possibilities that exist, or even a very small number of them. As long as I insist I know exactly where I'm going, I simply never see where else I might go. I limit myself to my view of the world. I'd had enough limitations. I wasn't willing to voluntarily impose more.

Remember Rita, my friend who lives around every limitation and who once had complete paralysis in her right shoulder and her arm and hand? As a result of her condition, her right arm hung lower at her side than is normal, and her right hand was closed with the wrist curved back toward her arm. Teaching her right shoulder, arm, and hand to respond has been a long, slow process. As Rita lay in her bed, she'd notice very small changes in the way her elbow was responding, or her shoulder or her hand. Although she couldn't immediately repeat the effect when she was standing up, she worked for months to be able to re-create the motions. Six months after first experiencing the sensation when lying down, Rita was able to re-create the movements while standing up. This process happened repeatedly — with Rita feeling the small motions while lying down and then learning over time to do them while standing up. Rita was changing her right arm one small goal at a time. Now, thirteen years after her strokes, Rita can turn her arm, move her elbow, hold her shoulders even, raise both her hands over her head, and open and close the fingers of her right hand.

Like Rita, I was discovering living with possibilities, but the stream of possibilities still had some rocks in it. I had other emotions to deal with besides the fear. Other feelings would get in the way of what I was doing.

## EMOTIONS ARE CLOSER TO THE SURFACE

There was, for me, a peculiar emotional quality to having a stroke. It felt as if a protective layer had been stripped away from me — as if I were exposed to the world without a buffer. I'd been in the hospital before for surgery. After surgery, for a while I'd regress and experience life in a more childlike state of helplessness. But having a stroke wasn't like that experience at all. Having a stroke was raw, as if my filters weren't in place.

First there was the emotional lability, or affect disorder. I hear that this disorder is now called *emotional incontinence* — not, in my opinion, a particularly kind term for those of us affected by it. It was just plain weird to get triggered and hysterically cry or laugh when I tried to talk. A seemingly small emotional response, a little feeling of tenderness or concern, would cause a big physical reaction. My head would shake. My eyes would stream with tears. My chest would heave. I could barely catch my breath. What was particularly challenging was the disconnect between what I was actually feeling and what I was expressing. Sometimes I would be quite calm emotionally while I cried and choked and couldn't speak. My sons coined a term for it. They called it *cryggling*, which is a cross between crying and giggling.

I tried to explain the phenomenon of seeming to express one thing while feeling another to the people who loved me. Bob and Fletcher and Jacob got it. My poor father didn't. He'd call. I'd try to talk, but I'd quickly sound hysterical simply because I was moved and touched that he had reached out to me. My father would get upset, and I had enough trouble talking when I wasn't crying so in the midst of my tears I'd have to hand the phone to somebody else. I felt so badly for my dad. He never understood that I wasn't nearly as uncontrolled as I sounded.

That affect disorder made it hard to be places with other people. One night in rehab, I went to see a film. I'm sure it was designed to be hopeful, but I found it difficult to watch. I quickly began crying uncontrollably. I'm certain I was a nuisance to the other patients in the room, but I couldn't help it. I sat there in the back of the rehab dining room watching this film, which started with a former Miss America who had experienced a stroke. She was walking. I wasn't. I was sitting in my wheelchair crying.

In addition to the affect disorder, with the filters gone everything was close to the surface. The fear and grief were there for sure, but also frustration, anger, simple sadness, jealousy, happiness, self-reproach, despair. All of it in a soup, immediate. It felt chaotic, and it was. I had to learn to live with it. It was as if my emotions had a quality of spasticity similar to the spasticity of my muscles.

Rehab provided no exercises to help me with this one. There was a social worker, but his main role was discharge planning and making sure my family had a realistic view of what living with me postrehab would be like. But I was still emotional. Because of the affect disorder, rehab sent me a neuropsychologist, who suggested I take medication to slow down the affects of the laughing and crying so I wouldn't upset my family. I tried one dose of the medication, but it made me feel even more disconnected than I was. That was enough of that. I told the neuropsychologist, "No, thank you," and explained that my immediate family was more okay with my laughing and crying than I was. And that was true.

My blessed family. I might have been spastic physically and emotionally, but they were there for me. Bob just wanted me back home in whatever condition I was in. I swear that man would have loved me no matter what. Fletcher, who lived far away, came back to visit me and called me and made me laugh and comforted me. Jacob, who lived closest to the rehab center, came to see me every other day, did my laundry, got me a blanket, and bought me pull-on pants to wear. Some families can't cope and have to send their family members to a nursing home. I was and am profoundly blessed to have the family I have.

I tried simply paying attention to the emotional soup to see if that would help in this case too. And it did. I was able to see that the emotions close to the surface were swirling around because of the stroke, not because I was crazy or emotionally unbalanced. Everyone has emotions. For me, poststroke, the emotions were just more volatile.

Most of the time I could see that, but the day Fletcher came to see me with Liam wasn't one of them. I hadn't permitted any of the grandchildren to be with me until then. Fletcher's oldest, Patrick, was in Seattle, and he was eight. Jacob's oldest, Alaric, was three. Liam was now eleven months and Jonah was two months. I was very concerned that my appearance would frighten the older ones.

Fletcher came, and I was so pleased to see him and happy to see Liam, although I felt sad because I couldn't hold him. But Liam was too young to know there was anything wrong with me, so at least I wasn't scaring him. The three of us visited in my room for a while, with me on the bed, Fletcher in a chair, and Liam in his stroller. I had a break for lunch and a rest between classes, but I had to go back to the gym in the afternoon and they had to leave.

When the time came for class, I needed to get out of bed and into my wheelchair. Fletcher helped with the transfer, and then off we went down the corridor together in the same direction, Fletcher pushing Liam, me pushing myself. The door to the rehab section of the hospital is quite close to the gym. At the door, Fletcher and Liam said good-bye — Fletcher with a sad expression on his face and Liam cheerfully oblivious in the way of small children everywhere. As I watched them go, I was filled with an overwhelming sense of feeling sorry for myself. In the midst of my swirling emotions, I measured myself against my grandson — never a productive thing to do.

I thought, "Here I am, fifty-five and in a wheelchair, wheeling about just like my eleven-month-old grandson. They're off to their lives, and I'm stuck in rehab struggling to do the simplest things. My grandson, at eleven months, is learning to walk, and so am I. I know he'll succeed, but I have no idea if I will." And I felt very envious, small and sad, and hopeless.

With a long face, I went to class — mats of course. The physical therapist noticed and asked me what was wrong. Fearing the affect disorder in the middle of the gym, I brushed her off and went to work, but the feeling didn't go away. Sad and dejected, I wheeled my way back to my room, where Perla noticed me.

Perla is a CNA, a certified nursing assistant, with a deep and generous heart, who was working in my section and had gotten to know me. She followed me to my room, helped me out of my wheelchair and into bed, and then sat on my bed with me. She took my hand in hers and began to talk from her heart. That day Perla reminded me of something very important as we talked about our lives. Perla too had an older husband. She had teenage kids at home. Her life had its own challenges, as everyone's does. Her husband was disabled. She was the primary breadwinner. She had issues to face.

What Perla reminded me that day is that, although I had problems, everyone else did too. I wasn't unique. I wasn't the only person who had challenges to deal with. The touch of Perla's hand and the sincerity of her sharing lifted my heart. Her simple act of kindness in the midst of my misery was priceless. Although I'd experience other episodes of feeling

sorry for myself in the time ahead, the memory of the touch
of Perla's hand has always kept me from falling so far into
despair again.

The emotional soup and the raw, unprotected feeling persisted for a long time. At first I found being with many people at once very taxing. I couldn't handle the emotional input
and the emotional tracking of that many themes. They were
too intense. It was as if a kind of skin had to be rebuilt. Knowing the value of working with small goals, I began to work on
rebuilding that skin in the same way I worked on lifting the
cookbook. I gradually started introducing more people at one
time into my life. I could talk with one, and then two, and
then three. As I did this, my emotional tracking abilities
improved.

Today, just as I have hyper-reflexive muscles on my left
side and trunk — more sensitive to stimulation than the right
side — I remain a little more emotionally available than many
people. Carol, my friend the therapist, and I talk about this
tendency. She experiences it too. For her it is an asset. She can
use that increased sensitivity to experience emotions, both her
own and other people's, as a tool in her group therapy sessions. Her ability to be so in touch with feelings gives permission and space for others to work with their own.

Carol has taught me that it's important to acknowledge
all the feelings, accept the volatility for what it is, and allow
the practice of working with small goals to gently build my
abilities. She has also taught me to seek help if I need it. Like
grief, repressed emotions can cause problems. The ordinary
ones come and go, sweep in and out, but sometimes after a

stroke people can suffer from chronic depression. The brain injury, upsetting the biochemical balance in the brain, may cause depression. Frustration and anger may cause depression. The point is it happens, so if signs of ongoing depression appear, get help. Recovery is contingent on work. Depression gets in the way of work. Get help if you need it, or if you see someone you love who needs it.

And there were still more things for me to learn.

# CHAPTER THIRTEEN

## *Habituating the Disability*

I WAS NOW BEGINNING TO BE ABLE TO FOCUS on something that my friend Stanley Keleman had explained to me: the concept of "learned nonuse."

Take a look at what you do, and see if you can identify how many habits appear in the space of a few hours. Habits are everywhere. Our bodies can turn anything into a habit. Before the stroke, I invariably put my pants on the same leg first every time. In fact, the habit was so ingrained that I still do it. Right leg first, followed by the left leg. It would be much easier, poststroke, if I did it the other way around. My right leg is more agile than my left, but I still put my pants on the way I've always done.

Our bodies and particularly our brains make habits to create efficiencies. We end up with hardwired brain circuits, predictable neural pathways, which are created when we do something over and over again. The brain says, "Oh, good, that action's solid and useful; I'll just reinforce it." While the brain is always remapping itself, teaching it to rewire a working section by challenging a habit takes a while. All of us who've tried to change a habit have the experience of how the habit reasserts itself unless we keep our attention on it and keep on trying to change it. The longer the habit persists, the harder it is to change.

The important and powerful thing to know about this is that the body and brain will habituate a disability quickly and will do so over and over again in different ways and different areas. It happens very fast. It's as if there's only so much that the brain wants to pay attention to at any one moment, and creating a habit will allow the brain to focus on something else. Creating a habit is a way of not having to pay attention.

That's what Stanley taught me. When he told me about learned nonuse, I began to watch for it. I saw how it worked. Habituation of the disability is one of the main reasons the statement that you only have a short time to recover is so self-predictive. Tell people they can't, the body makes a habit of the disability, and then they don't see themselves as able and they won't be able. If you don't take away anything else from this book, please remember this one observation: Our bodies will make a habit of a disability, and it's up to us to break those habits.

Nobody had told a man I met named George this information about habits. George had had a severe stroke. He worked very hard for a while and made good progress but then ran into a bunch of habits that his body had created. He thought the habits were permanent disabilities. Unfortunately, George believed that his habits and his disability were the same thing. Because he didn't know he could challenge the habits, he didn't challenge them and stayed stuck for a long time. Now that George knows that his body was making a habit of the disability, he has begun to work again and is finding new ways to move.

How many things do we all do that we've made a habit of and, because the habit takes some effort to change, we think we're stuck? I'll give you a simple rehab example. I learned to walk again. The standard brain-default foot position for starting to walk or walking with a brain injury is toe down first. Watch babies learning to walk. They put their feet down toe first. It's safer; it's easier to balance. That's the way I learned to walk again. I would place my left foot in front of me toe down first.

I could still be walking that way. It's not very efficient, but I could get anywhere I wanted to go. I could walk around the grocery store toe down first. I could go to the movies and walk down the aisle to my seat toe down first. Sometimes when I'm walking downhill on a slope and I'm feeling uneasy about my balance, I still do it. Watch yourself. You might notice that in uncertain terrain you might do it too.

But I was paying attention. I started looking at my left foot. Then I started looking at my right foot. Then I started watching other people walk. I asked myself, "What's normal?" I saw that what's normal is for people to do a heel strike first and roll through the foot in the stride. Heel comes down, momentum through the foot occurs and the toes touch last, not first. I looked at this and wondered, "Is the failure of my left foot to do this a disability? Do I have the muscle/brain connection to roll through from the heel to the toe?" I tried it. And I discovered that walking toe down first was a habit I was developing.

I actually had the ability to walk heel down first. I simply wasn't using it. I began to practice, reminding my left foot over and over again. It wasn't easy at first. Like most habits, I had to work at changing it. I still work at it since my walking gait is not yet completely restored, although most of the time I now do it semiautomatically. If I hadn't challenged the habit, I would still be walking toe down first, and by now it would be a deeply ingrained habit, much harder to change.

Observation and attention are keys here. My less affected side became my teacher. We can watch ourselves. If one part of us is more injured than the other, we all have a built-in teacher in our less injured parts. I modeled my behavior on what I observed my less affected side doing. The other place to look is at how a person who is not injured does something. Walking with someone who has a normal gait is a really helpful part of breaking habits for me. When I do that, particularly on the mountain, where it is quiet and I can hear the pattern of the footfalls of my companion, my body tries to imitate the rhythm of the sound as if I were making music with my footfalls. This challenges my body's own walking-gait habits.

Two sets of habits form and interlock. The weakened side makes a habit of staying weak, and the stronger side makes a habit of compensating for the weak side. The person most well known for working with this understanding is Edward Taub, who worked extensively with constraint-induced therapy, which I described earlier. He is the one who called the habituation *learned nonuse*. It was his work that Stanley Keleman told me about. Just understanding the concept was liberating for me. If I could learn "nonuse," I could learn use.

Taub taught that in order to break habits, we need to stop

the strong side from doing all the work. The more affected side will simply go along for the ride if the stronger side is handling the task. In order to stop the stronger side from working, sometimes we need to make it very clear that we're not using it. People may wear a mitten on their more able hand so the fingers of that hand can't do much, or they may put that hand in their pocket and leave it there so the arm doesn't move either.

Many of the compensatory patterns are hard to discover. It helps to ask the more affected side to do something unusual. I tried and still use Taub's technique of insisting the less able side work by refusing to use the more able side. Often I will intentionally do all the dishwashing work in the kitchen with my left hand, putting my right hand down and not using it, or I'll attempt to put my socks on with my left hand.

One stroke survivor, Peter, tries drawing with his affected hand. He had never tried to draw before the stroke, but now he goes to a drawing class to encourage his hand to try something new. As it was recovering, his hand remembered how to write words, but it had never experienced the movements that drawing requires. Holding a pencil to write and holding a pencil to draw are different actions, and the way the pencil moves to make a line is not the same as the way it moves to write a letter. Making a line that goes backward in relation to the writing motion is common in drawing. Peter's brain had to pay attention to what he was asking his hand to do and break habits to do it.

You never know where the habits will get ingrained, so new challenges are very useful. Some months ago my friend Betty Joan gave me some exercises to do to stretch my hips and knees, which have been developing arthritis. One of the exercises involves lying on my left side and bringing my right leg over my left with the knee bent and the right foot on the floor next to my left thigh. The stretching action is to lift my left leg toward the ceiling, a motion that calls for the inner thigh muscles to move the leg sideways.

The first time I tried this my left leg said, "What??? You want me to do what?" I had no idea at all how to initiate the motion. I had to watch my right leg do it over and over again before I could convince my left leg to try. Months later, I can now do this exercise fairly well, but clearly my left leg had habituated a movement pattern that didn't include knowing how to work those muscles in that direction. I would never have known this unless I'd tried the exercise Betty Joan gave me.

My friend Rita challenges her habits on a horse. She works with a physical therapist named Fran Judd in Cotati, who has combined her love of horses and her love of physical therapy in an establishment she calls the Renaissance Healing and Learning Center. The center, a lively place, full of caring people and animals, is located a short distance off the expressway. A barn and a covered, dirt-floor paddock meet the eye as you drive up the unpaved road. For those who find it hard to mount a horse, there's a platform with steps leading to a height that makes it easy to swing a reluctant leg over the horse's back. Gentle, patient, and seemingly aware of the good they do, the horses walk slowly around the covered area, led by volunteers and staff.

The center works with children who are autistic or who have cerebral palsy as well as with brain-injured adults. It's amazing to watch. As the horse walks, Rita performs various exercises on horseback, turning, reaching, opening her hand and arm. The rocking walking motion of the horse builds trunk strength and also challenges the ways Rita's left side compensates for her injured right side. Swaying and moving, Rita's muscles are called upon to try something new.

Another stroke survivor, Margaret, challenges her habits by walking on uneven ground. When she goes into the country to take a walk, she chooses a path that has rocks and slopes and turns and steps in it. Every time her feet are faced with a new surface or angle to step onto, she has to challenge the way her body moves. Sometimes she walks on the beach and gets her feet wet at the edge of the water, experimenting with the way the softness of the sand makes her legs move differently. Sometimes she takes her shoes off to feel new surfaces under her feet.

Another person in recovery, Herman, uses a little trampoline to help him break his habits. When Herman stands on the trampoline, touching a wall if he needs to in order to keep his balance, he can create unpredictable motion by gently moving his body. The surface of the trampoline shifts, and he has to try to find his balance and use his legs and trunk muscles in ways he hasn't tried before. The unpredictable motion creates a situation he can't respond to with a habit. By asking his body to move in new ways he challenges himself.

I was understanding how vital it was to start from where I was and pay attention to everything I was doing, particularly my habits, but I realized that I needed to be able to use this information wisely.

PART FOUR

# BEING SKILLFUL

# CHAPTER FOURTEEN

## *Believing in Change*

W HEN BOB AND I MARRIED, we held a simple ceremony
in the house, sitting together beside the windows. As
we faced each other, he asked for my hand. Into it he placed
a single rose, which he told me to hold gently, in an open
palm. He explained to me that to hold the rose tightly would
crush it. To hold it gently would allow it to breathe and
change. To keep our relationship healthy and joyful, he reminded me that it was important to understand that change
is the natural course of life — that our relationship wouldn't
stay the same. The rose was a symbol of that potential for
change, and whether cut or left on the bush, it would inevitably change too. The petals would unfold. Eventually
they would drop. The base of the flower would be all that
remained, and the bush would bloom again. Change would
come.

Change and transformation are always occurring. So
often we hold tightly to what we want, crushing it. Or we
push away what we fear so fiercely that we don't allow ourselves to experience the power of, and work with, the change
that's happening. How we accept and facilitate the changes in

our lives can determine whether we flourish or whether we stifle ourselves and our potential.

For me to take advantage of and to use the power of change, I have to believe two things: First, I have to believe that change is possible. Second, I have to believe that how I work with change makes a difference in what happens.

If I don't have these two beliefs, I won't try. If I don't try, I won't open to the possibility inherent in the change as it's occurring. Believing that a situation can transform and that I can have an impact on that transformation is crucial. The fastest way to close off possibilities is to make a decision in advance that something is impossible. I know; I've certainly done that to myself many times. Acknowledging and living around limitations, and refusing to try are two very different things. The willingness to live creatively around limitations is a constant demonstration of the belief that change is possible. Refusing to try often begins with an unexamined view of something, another form of hidden agenda.

Stroke recovery demonstrates the power of hidden agendas in a very tangible way. With stroke recovery, if people get discouraged and decide at some point that they are forever stuck, they stay stuck. Period. Positive change in stroke recovery only comes with effort. Effort only happens if we believe that there's some point to the effort. If we go through the motions of something because we think someone is making us do it against our will, we will tend to get very poor results with stroke recovery. The brain and body respond to our belief in and our desire to change.

We can use the practice of paying attention to discover

hidden agendas. If we notice that we're holding ourselves back from doing something, we can pay attention and wonder what might be stopping us. Every time we hear ourselves say, "This can't happen," or "I'll never be able to do that," we might discover that there's a decision or an opinion that's keeping us from opening to possibility. I never in a million years thought I would ever write a book. I admired people who did and thought to myself, "That will never be me. I'll never do that." So I didn't try. What was stopping me? It turns out that my hidden agenda all along has been that I didn't think I had anything to say that would be useful. This unexamined feeling resulted in a hidden decision never to let myself try to write. When I gave up that agenda, I opened to possibilities. I decided I would write this book and just see what happened.

All the stroke survivors I know who have worked on their recoveries and who make an effort to discover how to live with whatever limitations they have share the belief that change is possible. When Rita and I give presentations, we talk about the power of believing in change. When Rita comes with me to give a talk, we stand in front of people and demonstrate what we mean. By the end of the talk, everybody in the room is saying it. If we put "Believe change is possible" to music, it would be our theme song.

The last person I asked to tell me what the doctors are currently saying about stroke recovery was my friend Afi, who said that she was told she had eighteen months to make significant recovery changes. That's better than six months, but it's still wrong.

There's no reason to believe that change can't continue to occur for the rest of our lives. My experience suggests that recovery continues as long as we're willing to work at it. My strokes were seven years ago. I'm still changing. The habituation of the disability may make change more difficult as time passes — the spasticity and contraction of the muscles can make movement very challenging — but if you don't continue to try to change you will never know what you might be able to do. I've been told that the doctors don't want to "create false hope." That seems to me to be a very unfortunate attitude because it so often stops people from trying. I'm not saying that the doctors can or should guarantee a certain outcome. Guaranteeing a certain outcome is the enemy of transformation. The point is what my dear friend Betty Joan said so clearly to me back when I was in rehab: Nobody knows what's possible.

It's not that complete restoration of function can always be achieved or is the sole, or even the major, measure of success. Some people achieve complete restoration of function. I haven't. I've achieved a lot. Others will experience a recovery different from mine. Each recovery is unique. What's important is understanding that change and transformation are always possible, always happening. As my son Fletcher says, "It's not about getting back 75 percent of your old life. It's about having 100 percent of your new life." The potential for positive change is always there. As long as we're alive, we're changing. And as long as we're willing to put in the effort, we can have a profound impact on the nature of that change.

Rita is the master of ongoing change. Thirteen years post-stroke, Rita is still recovering, and she won't stop. I've known Rita two and half years now. When Rita's right hand didn't move and its fingers were curled shut, Rita could only open the fingers of her right hand if she pulled them open with her left hand. Last summer I watched Rita demonstrate to the group we were talking to how she can now open the fingers of her right hand. The movement is simple, not complete, but it's quite something to watch, and it keeps improving.

As you may recall, thirteen years ago Rita was told that she might someday walk with a quad cane; she now delights in doing a deep squat raising both her arms over her head. Her balance is perfect. Her right arm doesn't quite come up as far as the left, but nearly. That arm was paralyzed for years. I don't know where that arm will be by next year, but I'm willing to bet that there will be positive change. The joy of watching Rita work on her recovery gladdens my heart. I remember the day I got the phone message about her first really long hike. She was exuberant. That was before our trip to the falls. Now that she can hike nine and a half miles, I wonder what the next adventure will be. I can't wait to hear what new challenge she has posed for herself. Rita refuses to give up. She refuses to listen to anybody tell her what she can and cannot do. She works on her physical abilities constantly, and she continues to improve her speech.

She isn't alone. My friend Cecilia didn't drive for ten years after her stroke. Cecilia is an artist who lives in a little town north of here with her teenage son. When you have a brain injury, the State of California pulls your driver's license.

While this policy isn't unreasonable, it does make it necessary to take a written test and a driving test before you can
have your license restored.

Cecilia had to rely on paratransit for ten years — vans
that come and take a disabled person to the doctor, to the
store, for a visit, or wherever the person needs to go. Paratransit is a truly great service and keeps people who can't
drive from being housebound, but it can be frustrating. It can
take a lot of time to coordinate waiting for a pickup and
return. Cecilia tells funny stories about her paratransit experiences. But all the while Cecilia was gratefully using paratransit, she never gave up on her desire to drive. Finally, after
ten years of work on her recovery, Cecilia felt confident
enough in her abilities to take driving lessons. She promptly
passed her test. Now she can drive herself to art school. I don't
know what kind of painter Cecilia was before her stroke, but
I can tell you that now she produces some of the most lyrical,
beautiful landscapes you can imagine. Having a stroke has not
stopped Cecilia from continuing to improve her artistic skills.
Cecilia is transforming.

Jeff had a stroke twenty years ago. After his stroke, when
he was able, he earned his teaching certificate and now teaches
the fourth grade. Jeff is so well loved and regarded for his
teaching that he wins awards as Teacher of the Year. With an
uneven walking gait and incomplete function in his left hand,
he has cheerfully thrown himself into the joys of working
with nine-year-olds. But there was still something missing in
Jeff's life. Before he had his stroke he'd been a musician,
playing his guitar and singing. Busy with his teaching, Jeff

put his music aside until this past year. Now he has begun to play his guitar again.

At first Jeff's left hand was unable to form the chords accurately enough and change position fast enough to play the songs that he wanted to sing, so he began to play using open tuning. Open tuning does not require a lot of left hand work, and Jeff could play songs using a plastic tube on one finger of his left hand, something called *slide guitar*. But as much happiness as this has brought Jeff, the story doesn't end with the slide. Since Jeff has picked up his guitar again, his left hand is becoming ever more dexterous, and Jeff is increasingly able to form chords. Recently he was asked to spend an evening in a local club singing backup for a friend of his. As Jeff is learning, there seems to be no limit to the time that change may be possible after a stroke.

## KEEP IT MOVING

Sometimes it takes a lot of effort and a long time to make something happen. For example, a man named Henry had a stroke that left his left arm and hand completely unresponsive. No matter how much Henry thought about his left arm, nothing happened. No movement. Nothing. From the shoulder blade all the way to the ends of his fingers, there wasn't a single response. But Henry had learned something very important. He knew that as long as his hand and arm weren't doing anything, he was in danger not only of habituating the disability but also of having the joints on his arm and hand get really stiff and frozen from lack of activity. Day after day, with no sign of response, Henry worked his left arm and hand, stimulating the muscles, bending the joints, keeping them flexible. When he'd walk, the arm would hang uselessly by his side or he'd carry it with his right hand. Rolling over in bed, Henry had to be very careful not to injure his left arm; he had to move it with his right arm so it didn't get caught underneath him and end up strained.

Most people might have given up after the first year, and the rest certainly would have given up after the second. But Henry isn't most people. Henry refused to give up. He worked his arm and hand. He kept them stimulated. He kept the joints flexible. Three years after Henry's stroke, he began to see the signs of movement in his left arm and hand. He kept working. He's still working. Now Henry can raise his left arm to his face and open the fingers enough to grasp things. If Henry had listened to the voices that told him he only had so much time to recover, whether it was six months or eighteen months, he would have given up and not have movement now. What Henry knew to do was to keep the affected side moving and stimulated — an absolutely essential principle. Without the movement, Henry's brain would never have responded, and the joints would have stiffened up into painful inflexibility.

Carol, my friend the therapist, keeps herself moving in another way. While she has function in all her limbs, she still has shaking in her left side along with some balance issues. Unwilling to stop moving and challenging herself, Carol has been exploring a movement method invented by Moshé Feldenkrais. Carol finds that the Feldenkrais practice creatively calls her muscles and brain into a new kind of action.

She's retraining, challenging, and healing her deficits even now, more than twenty years after her stroke.

Because of who Carol is and the way she uses what she learns to benefit others, she isn't content to simply work on this practice for herself. Carol is taking training courses so that she can teach other people these techniques, and she introduces Feldenkrais principles into the group work she leads. With her clients week in and week out, Carol sets the example and holds forth the possibility of ongoing change.

All of these friends of mine demonstrate the willingness to be open to possibility coupled with a wonderful, stubborn persistence. That's what it takes.

# CHAPTER FIFTEEN

## *Skillfulness and Persistence*

Recovery is hard work. Period. Rewiring a brain doesn't happen by sitting around. This isn't like recovering from the flu. Drinking lots of fluids and plenty of bed rest will keep you hydrated and rested, but it won't teach you to walk.

I've never worked as hard in my life as I did in the rehab center. I was exhausted most of the time. At the end of every day it was all I could do to go to the dining room and eat. Some nights I begged the nurses to bring me my dinner in bed. Usually in the middle of the day when I had a break for lunch, I'd eat in my room and try to take a short nap before going back to the gym or to speech or OT — wherever I was headed next. Five days a week I had an appointment with Erwin, with Kam, with Tav, with Julia, with the mat therapists. Saturdays were half days, and we often worked in group classes in OT and speech.

I told Erwin I would volunteer for any classes that were being taught to the interns so I could work with the therapists while they demonstrated to the students. Some mornings I'd get up earlier than usual and be part of just such a class. In my room, I couldn't get up by myself, but I could do hand exercises in the bed and all the peculiar facial stretches that Kam taught me to help my speech improve, so I did.

I worked and worked for two and a half weeks, then asked that my time at rehab be extended, and it was. Because I was working so hard and because I was showing progress, I was given an additional week. I was elated. I would have stayed in rehab longer if I could have, but competition for space in the rehab center is a fact of life. Other people needed to be there to allow them to start their recoveries, and eventually I was given a date certain when I would go home.

To prepare for my coming home, my family attended classes to learn necessary skills. There was a lot for them to learn so they could work with me safely, particularly how to transfer me in and out of a car and how to drive the wheelchair over curbs. They would have to know what they could expect of me, what I could and couldn't do.

Before I could go home, there were two things I absolutely had to learn. Julia had to teach me how to walk on steps, and Erwin had to teach me how to get off the floor. I'd bounded up and down stairs with little thought just a few weeks previously. I'd carried laundry without paying much attention to where my feet were as they found each step and turned in the staircase with assurance and ease. Now I was in the gym gazing across the room, in the opposite direction from the parallel bars, at the stairs I would have to master. This was a simple, straight up-and-down staircase with big railings, consisting of a wooden set of six stairs up, a small platform, and six stairs down. I looked at those stairs with

Julia by my side and had no idea how to begin. It was time for my first lesson, and she wheeled me across the room to the edge of the stairs and had me stand.

Fortunately for me, Julia had taught this many times before. As with one-handed shoe tying, there's a specific technique for going up and down stairs with one disabled side. The disabled foot goes up last. Right foot up. Bring the left foot up to meet it. Right foot up. Left to meet it. And the other way around for down. Disabled side down first. Left down. Bring the right down to meet it. Left down. Bring the right down to meet it. Grab the railing securely. Take your time. It was slow, and I was plenty nervous. My legs were uncertain, remembering the way I'd walked stairs a few weeks before. Now trying to process new instructions and stay safe, after many attempts I got the idea and carefully focused on the practice so I wouldn't put myself at risk when I was at home. Stairs are scary when you're no longer confident in your ability to race up and down them.

Erwin's teaching was harder to learn. Once I was home, it was possible that I would fall. If I fell and nobody was around, I'd have to be able to get off the floor myself. I had been a floor sitter before the stroke. If there was a project to do that required me to spread out, I promptly sat on the floor and started to work.

Now the floor looked like impossible terrain. I was just learning to stand and to walk. I couldn't imagine getting on the floor. If I hadn't developed so much trust in Erwin, I'm not sure I could have been persuaded to try what he asked of me. First, in order to learn how to get up, I had to get down.

I sat on the edge of one of the raised mats off in the corner of the gym near the staircase as Erwin told me to slide myself down. I really didn't want to do this. Really.

Eventually, with a great deal of struggle and effort, I was lying on the floor. I was in a panic. I could barely register what Erwin was saying as he gave me instructions. He wasn't going to do this for me. I was having to find some way to do it for myself, rolling on my side, pushing off, finding a way to get on my knees, bringing my right foot up under me. This was serious business — so many things to do at once and so much of me still not responding to my mental instructions. Finally, barely, I made it back up to sitting on the raised mat. Erwin being Erwin insisted I do this three or four more times. It was overwhelmingly difficult and exhausting, but I had to learn it.

I swore I would never fall so I would never have to get up off the floor. What I didn't realize at the time was that I was going to have to use the ability to get on and off the floor to do my exercises once I got home. I didn't live in a rehab gym. I bought an exercise mat, but I had no raised table to put it on. Erwin's teaching that day came in very handy, like every-thing else I learned at rehab.

The day came to go home. I was packed up, placed in the wheelchair, and brought to the curb outside the hospital entrance. Time to use the transfer instructions for how to get out of a wheelchair and into a car. Stand up. Hold on to the door, turn, squat, bottom in first, reach back to touch the seat and stabilize, and then swing in the legs. I needed my right hand to help my left leg into the car. Finally I was loaded into the car, and Bob drove me away from the hospital toward home. We drove across the top of the bay as the sense of new beginnings began to arise in my heart.

There was plenty to be happy about. I was alive. I was going home. I'd made progress in the rehab center, and I was determined to work at it and make more progress. I didn't know how much I could do, but I was ready to keep trying. To savor the beginning of this new chapter, out on my own without the therapists and nurses, and to celebrate all that I'd achieved so far, we stopped at the drive-in and had ice-cream cones halfway home. June, the taste of ice cream in my mouth, warm sun coming through the windows of the car onto my face — a new part of my life was indeed beginning.

Up onto the mountain we came. As we crested the hill, I looked to my left. Below us spread the bay, and though I couldn't see the detail with my unfocused eyes, I could still appreciate the broad outline of the expanse of water glowing as if lit from within. As we turned onto the main road that runs along the spine of the mountain, I could smell the trees — that heady scent of eucalyptus and evergreen. Both elated and scared, I took as deep a breath as I could and inhaled the fragrance as we drove along that steep little street, turned into the gravel parking area, and brought the car as close to our small gray and blue house as possible. Back into the wheel-chair, and I was pushed to the door and helped up the two steps into the kitchen.

There I was — home. Looking around, I smiled. I was scared, but being home still felt great. I'd gained some confidence during my two home visits, and I thought I might find a way to manage the challenges somehow. Jacob had come over and installed handicapped bars in the downstairs bathroom and additional grab bars and supports on the way down the stairs. Bob had put my bed in the living room. Family was there to help. I was home. Now what?

Now I would organize my days in earnest. Being home didn't mean I could stop working as hard as I was able. Now that I was home the rest of the work began. No more gym. No more routine set by someone else. Occasional visits back to see Erwin on an outpatient basis, but no more daily appointments. Now I had to determine the schedule, and I couldn't slack off. I had seen the results of hard work. I knew that if I didn't continue to work that hard, I wouldn't be giving myself the best chance I could.

To be effective, the work must be skillful, persistent, focused, and intense. Edward Taub, who popularized constraint-induced therapy, taught that intense, focused practice is what makes the difference. This is not so different from a musician or a professional athlete. They become excellent at what they do because they work and work and work in a very focused way. Musicians play scales for hours, limbering up and training their responses to the instrument.

I couldn't just say: "Oh, I'll work half an hour on Tuesday and then maybe again on Thursday." Rehab had sent me home with specific exercises. I needed to schedule time every day — not just occasionally but every day — to do my exercises and do them thoroughly. I couldn't just race through them as I'd tried to do early on in mats class; I needed to do them slowly and completely, with my attention focused on every movement. If I didn't devote that kind of energy and intention, my brain wouldn't get the message that this was important, and it wouldn't devote the needed resources to the effort. In rehab, the therapists had helped keep me focused. At home, that responsibility was mine alone.

Doing my exercises every day was critically important, but regular practice wasn't enough. I needed to be skillful, to work smart. My entire house, the property, and the mountain became my gym. Literally everything I did was an opportunity to work on my rehab, if I approached it that way. I'd watched my therapists closely. I had learned and was learning everything I could from them, and I was watching both my own body and the way other people moved. I could learn to use any action in a skillful way to work on my recovery.

Being skillful is not something we start out with. Thinking that we have to know how to do something before we begin is another hidden agenda that closes off possibilities. Today I can look at the financial situation of a small company and understand the books and how the money works. When I started as a bookkeeper trainee in the law firm, I knew nothing about double-entry bookkeeping, the basis for all accounting systems. Nothing. I learned as I went along. When I worked for the neighborhood-shopping-center developer, he let the bookkeeper go one day and told me I was now in charge of the financial statements, the computer, and the record keeping — the works. I had no idea how to do *all* that, so I bought an accounting textbook. Every morning I would get up early to read a chapter before I got the boys ready for school and went off to work, praying that what I'd learned so far would be enough to get me through. Over time I learned more.

Being skillful is simply doing the very best we can with what is in front of us at any given moment and being willing to learn. Doing our best — that's all. We don't have to be anything more than we are. We just need to pay attention, do our best, and stay open to learning. Who we are is enough.

Using what I had — including the mindfulness practice and attention I'd been cultivating — helped me stay focused and look closely at every action, no matter how small. How did I get my socks out of the drawer in my dresser? What part of that could I do right now? How could I do something differently — even a little bit differently? Each time I tried an action, I learned something new about how I could do it and what I might do the next time I tried it. I asked myself the question "How can I remember that it's the small goals that make a difference?" If I could grasp the socks in my left hand and found that pulling them out of the drawer was partially possible, I would work to bring them out a little farther the next time and the next, until I could pull them all the way out.

In a funny way, persistence became harder the more function I regained. At the beginning when so little was possible, every new achievement was a delightful surprise and a cause for celebration. After a while, when I'd achieved what felt like, and clearly was, a lot of positive change, I could see how many differences were still apparent between what I could do and what I wanted to do. When the gross motor skills were in place, I was left with the myriad of smaller things: the balance, the strength, the coordination, the fine motor skills.

There were so many skills to learn. When those skills seemed so near and yet so far, I became discouraged, frustrated, and worn-out from the effort. The taste of the freedom of moving without thought — the freedom of being able to reach for things without clumsiness — the flavor of that freedom was almost in my mouth but not quite there. And yet, if I were to succeed and train past the disability, I would have to keep on trying.

How would I keep myself motivated? Working at home brought the opportunity to do new things, to try approaches to healing that I hadn't been able to access in rehab. And to stay motivated, I would have to call on my creativity.

# CHAPTER SIXTEEN

## *Being Creative*

NEUROPLASTICITY STUDIES HAVE SHOWN that novelty stimulates the brain. That makes intuitive sense. When we do the same thing over and over again without change, our attention falters, our motivation weakens. We get bored.

I was working hard, but I never could have kept up that pace unless the work had become fun in some way. Maybe some people are disciplined enough to work relentlessly on something that's dry and repetitive, but I'm not. I like novelty. To make this work for me, I needed to use my creative juices to make it interesting.

Everything can be treated as a puzzle, an opportunity for a new solution. If we look at something as a burden and a trial — something we have to do — and nourish resentment toward it, we shut down creativity and with it, joy. Dr. Ruth Richards has edited a wonderful book called *Everyday Creativity and New Views of Human Nature*. In her introduction to the book, Richards writes of applying creativity to our daily lives: "It can pull blinders from our eyes, and bring us alive, making us more conscious participants. . . . It can offer us joy, energy, and challenge."

I needed to see the challenges of dealing with my life as if it were a puzzle I could find a way to solve — a call to creativity. Some days I was more successful at this than others. On those days I felt positive and encouraged. Other days, I needed to feel and then let go of the anger, grief, and frustration. I strove for the satisfaction of creativity, but whatever I was feeling, my job was to keep on working with what I had. On the days when fun was nowhere in sight, I didn't give up. I tried again the next day to find ways to enjoy what I was doing.

Once I was home, I tried all sorts of things I couldn't do in the hospital. The choices I made were particular to me, to what I know and have experience with. What I did is an example, not a prescription. What we try isn't as important as introducing novelty and finding a joyful way to be creative with what we do. A woman at one of my talks told me she had recovered from a stroke by going bowling. I don't bowl, but I can see how that would be a great idea. Another used gardening as a way to delight and motivate herself. A man I met is eager to go home and work with his horses, and another to get back to his machine shop. Two examples from the many creative efforts of the friends I mentioned earlier are Cecilia and Henry: Cecilia uses her painting, and Henry uses his work. Whatever works to keep us encouraged and engaged, and to introduce new ways to challenge the body, can be helpful.

I love acupuncture. If you haven't tried it, you might think being stuck with needles is a weird thing to love, but the flow of delicious energy it produces in me feels so good. Acupuncture is a science of the body that has been practiced for many thousands of years. The acupuncturist I see is both a Western-trained physician and an acupuncturist. Using acupuncture he has helped people with conditions ranging from colds to cancers. Even before I had my strokes, he had been a source of tremendous help to me in many ways, including the time I had a frozen shoulder. And Rita, who was herself trained as an acupuncturist, tells me that early in her rehabilitation, she had many regular acupuncture treatments that proved pivotal in the recovery of her speech. We both continue to use acupuncture to support our ongoing healing.

My goal was to reestablish a connection that was broken in my electrical system — my brain wasn't talking effectively with my body. Acupuncture works with the nervous system, so what better way to stimulate the possibilities for reconnection of my brain to my body than through acupuncture? Since I love acupuncture so much, this was an easy choice. I found the stimulation, particularly of my left side, remarkably helpful.

Marty Rossman, the deeply kind and talented doctor I've seen over the years for acupuncture, is also a guided imagery specialist. Guided imagery is designed to encourage a creative response to whatever is happening. Since I could do guided imagery lying down, this was something I could try in rehab.

Guided imagery calls on the deep wisdom we each have within ourselves. When we use guided imagery, we allow ourselves to be quiet and peaceful and ask our psyche to guide us by bringing up an image or images that may help us direct our healing. This is often easiest to do if we have the words of a guide helping us relax, either someone present in the room, or a voice on a recording. Betty Joan, who is trained in guided imagery work and uses it in her medical practice, invited me to try it when she saw me. She led me through a short process to get me started. There have been many studies on guided imagery, and many tapes and CDs are available to help guide those who are new to the work.

At the time, I was very concerned about my inability to focus my eyes. I knew I could work tangibly on my walking, but I was at a loss for a way to work on my eyes. Betty Joan suggested I allow an image to arise in my mind related to this concern. My image came from what I knew. I'd been in the real estate business. I like construction equipment. There was a "spill" in my brain. So the image that came to me was of very, very tiny backhoes and graders and dump trucks busily clearing away the spilled blood from my brain. Up and down and over and under the overpasses of the blood vessels, these minute vehicles worked at clearing away the mess. I loved the image. It was both funny and useful. I worked with the image lying in my bed, evening after evening.

Knowing more now about the power of neuroplasticity and attention, I have no doubt that focusing on a healing image encouraged my body to respond. There's clear evidence that using this kind of imagery provokes a biological response in the body. Did my image help my brain heal? I can't say for sure, but there's no doubt that I have my vision back.

When I returned home, my body was longing for touch and for stretching, so I tried massage and a wonderful practice called the Rubenfeld Synergy Method, invented by my friend Ilana Rubenfeld. All the contact and movement involved in these practices and the emotional release and relearning in the Rubenfeld Synergy Method sent messages to my brain not to forget about the parts of me that weren't functioning and to embrace them. As I lay on the massage table or the bed, the person working with me could move parts of me that I couldn't yet move. This felt so nourishing. My body loved the touch and the movement. All the while the contact was telling my brain that these parts of me were still important.

I was learning to move in ways that allowed me to walk and cook and dress and get in and out of the car, but these movements still didn't challenge all the muscles and coordination in my body. What else could I do? I wasn't yet stable enough for something like dancing, but I wanted to try moving in ways that were different and new, that presented another kind of challenge. I tried a very simple form of ch'i kung designed for people recovering from illnesses. Ch'i kung comes from the traditions that created martial arts and tai chi, and involves movement and breathing exercises that are designed to be therapeutic. I still practice ch'i kung. The exercises challenge me to move gracefully in ways that are out of the ordinary range of my usual movements. When I do them, I become calmer and move more fluidly.

Sometimes my body felt strained and out of balance as I moved. I tried chiropractics, to see if that would help. Eventually I found my way to an extraordinary chiropractic doctor named Robert Adamich. The gentle stretching, stimulation, energy release, and body positioning he does with me invite my body to be healthy and remind it what it's like to be balanced. I continue to see Dr. Adamich, and his work with me helps break the compensation patterns that develop when my right side tries to do the work of the left side.

Those were some of the practices and outside influences that helped support what I was doing, but as Dr. Ruth Richards reminds us, the opportunity for creativity arises in each moment in our everyday lives. I found that carrying a glass of water was a way to make a game out of working with my left side. My left side had and still has more vibration in it than it did before the strokes. The muscles wobble when they work. Carrying a glass of water in my left hand makes tiny tidal waves in the glass, which bounce off one another and the sides of the glass. The result can be a great sloshing of water on the floor. It would be much easier to carry the glass in my right hand, but it wouldn't be as much fun. There would be no game, no creative challenge, as I learn to control the waves so the water stays in the glass.

And the mountain where I live, and all of its varied challenges, has become my constant creative stimulus. The mountain is beautiful, and it never lets me off easy. It calls me and it challenges me. Some of the challenges are fun, and some are frustrating. One night some months after my return home, my friend Sara was visiting and we discovered that we had left something in the car. By then I'd learned to very carefully walk to the garage over the gravel in broad daylight. But now it was late at night and dark. Realizing that I didn't dare to walk to the garage after dark, even with the path lights on, I sat in the kitchen crying tears of frustration. I was still way too uncertain of my footing and balance at that point. I felt trapped and frustrated that night, but the mountain had laid down the challenge. I would — I repeat I *would* — learn to walk to the garage after dark. And I have.

The mountain is full of creatures: the deer who would stare at me wide-eyed and then bound away, the raccoons who would dump the garbage if we didn't keep it in locked bins, the squirrels who would chuck at me ceaselessly from the trees, the possums and the lizards and the birds and my sleek and agile cat, Sam. I was worried when I left rehab that Sam wouldn't welcome me home the way I was — that he'd find me too odd to understand, that he'd be frightened and avoid me. I shouldn't have worried. I could sit. I could make a lap. I was still useful as far as he was concerned.

Sam knows exactly what he wants and what he likes and is more than willing to let you know what that is. Expression, gesture, and voice are the tools he uses to make sure you're *absolutely* clear what he wants from you. *Inscrutable* is not a word to use to describe Sam. You generally have a very good idea of what's on his mind and if, by chance, you're being unreasonably dense, he'll persist until you get the message. I tried petting Sam with my left hand. He let me know immediately if my fingers were doing a satisfactory job and made it abundantly clear what he thought of my efforts. His reactions were a constant guide to making the motions of my fingers more subtle.

Other people recovering from strokes find their own uniquely creative paths to recovery. Rita worked with the constraint induced therapy popularized by Edward Taub. This is the practice that insists the less able side participate in the recovery by restraining the more able side. One of the practices Rita tried was to restrain her left arm and use her right arm to write on a piece of paper. In order to do this, she put a very large piece of paper on a table, anchored down the edges, and grasped a very large pen in her right, paralyzed, hand, then wrote her name in huge letters. Now she has the paper size down to regular letter size, and her writing has become more and more legible.

The point is that everything has the potential to be a creative challenge if we approach it that way. I encountered both the creative challenge that served the rehab process and the challenge of developing the art of living around my limitations. I found I could look at each thing I couldn't yet do as a loss or as an opportunity to find a new way to do something. That was my choice. The facts of the situation were the same whether I approached it as a way to nourish my defeat, focusing on what I'd lost, or saw it as an opportunity to employ my creativity and find a way to get it done.

Don't assume in advance that a given activity will be useless. You never know what will work. My friend Afi had a brain injury — a CVA, or cardiovascular accident; Afi says the doctors haven't yet quite figured out the exact nature of it. The result of the injury was that Afi's left leg and arm were paralyzed. By the time Afi left rehab, she had begun to be able to walk with a cane, but her left arm was still completely paralyzed and also had no sensation. Afi is left-side dominant, so the loss of her left arm and hand presented some significant challenges.

A month or so after Afi's discharge from rehab, her

doctor suggested that Afi get an MRI to look again at what might have happened in her brain. As she lay in the MRI tube, Afi decided to support her left arm by holding her left hand in her right during the test. If you've ever been in an MRI tube, you know that they are close, noisy, and full of intense vibrations. Afi reports that during the test her left arm felt as if there were jolts of electricity running down it. The experience was so painful and frightening that Afi almost asked for the test to be stopped, but she decided to stick with it until the end.

A couple of days after the MRI, Afi's hand began to experience sensations. Two weeks after the test, Afi was able to use both the hand and the arm. She called her doctor and asked him to put her in the MRI tube the other way around to help her legs. He refused to believe that the MRI had anything to do with the recovery of function in her hand and arm. But why not? Who knows?

Recent discoveries in brain function have revealed that the ability to sing and the ability to speak come from different areas of the brain. A person with the type of profound aphasia that my friend Rita experienced at the beginning may still be able to sing songs with words in them. Rita sang. The words were in the songs. She tells everyone we meet who has aphasia that singing might help bring the words back into speech.

Music can have many benefits. My strokes took place seven years ago. Last year, I began singing again; while I didn't have aphasia, I discovered that the music challenges a kind of deliberateness, a nonspontaneous quality, which has gotten ingrained in the way I move since the stroke. With the beat of the music, my left foot starts keeping time, and my body sways and responds. I can feel the flexibility increase.

Don't stop. Keep on trying new things. Fill your life with possibilities. Until you try it, you won't know what will help.

*...Disability*

I received was to
... I went home was
... ased on the abilities
... sk I tried called for

? While the parts of
... vere learning how to
... se of what I could do
... nore coordinated. To
... I began to train and
... prestroke strength. I'd
... ne more fit if I could.
... Before the stroke, I'd
... nk strength I had. After
... f me that were trying to
... k stronger than before.
... st my left leg as it tried to
... ght. Doing bridging and
... capacity to walk while the
rest of me was ... and coordination.

This is what I call *training past the disability*. The idea is to become stronger and more able than I was before the stroke, in whatever ways possible. The idea is also to create an ongoing development of a new dynamic balance in my body. My body is always seeking to be in balance. As I strengthen one part, the point of balance shifts. Finding a new balance as I was healing wasn't a process I could force. It wasn't a process of efforting. It was a process of being. As I healed and found new ways to stabilize myself, to strengthen and to function, my dynamic balance shifted.

One man I met named Arthur wanted to drive his car after his stroke, but he still had weakness and paralysis in his right hand. Working with his OT to find adaptive equipment, Arthur learned about putting a knob on his steering wheel to allow him to drive safely with one hand while he continued to work on the recovery of his weaker hand. Doing all the work of driving with one hand can be difficult. In order to be able to drive safely, Arthur strengthened his left arm and hand by lifting weights and practicing the motions that would be required when turning the steering wheel. As a result, Arthur's left arm and hand have grown considerably stronger than they were before the stroke.

Another stroke survivor, Nancy, wasn't much of an athlete before her stroke. She took walks but not long ones, and spent more time in front of her computer or reading a book than getting exercise. After her stroke, Nancy realized that she was going to have to change her approach to exercise because she needed to depend on some parts of her body to do most of the work for a while. Her response to this challenge was to get into her local pool and begin walking in the water. The water-walking did two things. First, it buoyed her up, making it easier to keep her balance as she learned how to stabilize herself. Second, it strengthened her legs and trunk muscles as she moved against the resistance in the water. The increased strength and coordination have allowed Nancy to travel for her job while she continues to work on her rehabilitation.

Training past the disability required me to pay attention and make sure that I didn't allow the parts that need to be challenged to take a free ride. That's when the disability habituates. What was necessary was to strengthen the less affected side — in my case, the right side — enough to help the other side without letting the other side give up the effort to change and improve.

I wanted to help my left side. I wanted to live around my limitations and give myself enough strength to do things, but I didn't want to let my left side off too easy. If I did, my brain would forget about it and go off to do more productive things. It was up to me to watch what I was doing and make sure my left side was challenged. As I gained strength and came closer to full functioning, remaining aware of this fact became ever more important. It would have been very easy to settle for almost enough, to stop training past the disability when I could more or less do things. I needed to keep on training and keep on strengthening past the point where I could get things done, and continue all the way to the point where I could do them in a balanced way. There's so much to learn and observe about what it means for the body to be in balance.

Carrying the pots from the stove gave me an opportunity. In the beginning, most of the work of carrying the pots was done by my right side, but my left side had to participate too and put in as much strength as it could. No slacking. Every time I lifted a pot, I tried to discover just how much of the work the left side could do. What could the hand grasp? What could the arm lift? The trick was to take it to the edge and no further — just enough — not so much that I would hurt myself but enough that my left arm and hand would get the message that they had work to do too.

One day when I was using a little hand vacuum, I decided to let my left hand try to do the work. At first my left hand was puzzled. I'd never asked it to run the vacuum before the stroke. What was I doing? I was making sure that my left hand never forgot that it was going to have to get back to work.

The body needs to be addressed in balance for both sides to work. Sometimes the weaker side needs to be addressed directly. Sometimes we can watch and notice that the stronger side is doing too much of the work and needs to let go of some of the effort in order to break its compensation patterns. When a man named Tom first learned to stand and try to walk poststroke, he didn't trust his weaker side and wouldn't put much weight on it. Later he realized that he had created a different compensation pattern. Tom noticed that he was putting more of his weight on the weaker side and less on the stronger side, because his stronger side was trying to always be ready to move. When he practiced deliberately shifting his weight from one side to the other while standing and then while walking, Tom began to change the compensation patterns. The unwinding of so many patterns of compensation is fascinating; there's so much we aren't aware of until we begin to challenge ourselves.

There are many ways people can train past their disabilities. Mike is a guy's guy, active, strong, and athletic. His stroke affected his left side, particularly his left hand. At first Mike concentrated only on working with his left hand, but after a while he realized that he was not maximizing what he could do, so he began to strengthen the rest of him beyond the level of strength he'd had before the stroke. Mike likes to play golf. He worked with a golf coach to increase the ability of his right arm and to add to the rotation of his body so that he could play golf one-handed. Last week, as he delights in saying, he played a better round of golf one-handed, with a lower score, than he'd ever achieved when he was playing two-handed before his stroke.

Mike also likes to go duck hunting. To be accurate and hold the gun steady, most people use two hands. Although Mike's left hand is improving, it isn't ready to help him shoot or play golf, so Mike has worked on strengthening his trunk muscles so he can use them instead of his left hand to help his right hold the gun steady. Putting on his waders, Mike goes off into the woods to hunt ducks, and happily shares the results of his accurate shooting with his family and friends.

## ENDURANCE

Strength is one part of what's required. The other part is endurance. Once I was back on the mountain with all its challenges, I needed to work, and I needed to manage my endurance while I strengthened. The trouble I'd had with sleeping was a thing of the past. Even with the bed in the middle of the living room, I could fall asleep with Bob sitting near me watching television. By the end of each day, I was so tired that staying awake was the problem, not staying asleep.

As soon as I was home, I began taking care of Bob again in whatever way I could. He was amazing, generous, and loving, but he needed some time and care and attention too. Having learned about kitchen safety and cooking from Tav, I began to prepare simple meals for us both. What had been so effortless that I'd barely noticed doing it before, such as preparing something as simple as a sandwich, was now a major aerobic event. By the time I put the food on the plates, I could barely muster the energy to eat it.

Reaching full endurance took me several years. As I healed and strengthened, I'd reach what felt like a stopping point — a level of endurance that was less than before my strokes, but more than at the beginning of the recovery process, and more than the last stopping point I'd reached. After a while at this level of endurance, if I kept training, I'd discover that what had seemed like a stopping point was simply a plateau. My body would consolidate the energy for a while, then build endurance to a new plateau.

Going home and facing the reality of what I could and couldn't do, and the limits of my endurance, helped me appreciate what I had to do to heal the injury to my brain. Besides all the work of rewiring my brain and providing appropriate challenges to stimulate it, I needed to remember that my brain had sustained a grave injury and would need time and rest to heal.

Part of the measure of the healing and the level of endurance I was building was the amount of input my brain could take. If several things were happening at once, my brain couldn't cope. I would overload. About eighteen months after my strokes, I remember attempting to attend a meeting where a lot of people were talking. The meeting lasted two hours. It was overwhelming for me. I was exhausted for two days afterward.

Now I work with organizations and recently ran a meeting with twenty people that started at 8:00 AM and finished at 5:00 PM. The subject was challenging, the group was diverse, with people expressing many differing points of view, and I loved every minute of it.

Now I have more endurance than ever, more than I ever imagined I would have again, but I have to work to maintain it. I've discovered since my strokes that if I slack off on my exercise routine I lose ground more rapidly than I did before the strokes. To stay fit, I have to keep working and to train myself more than before. It may have something to do with the fact that I'm older, but I think it has more to do with the strokes.

Walking, which I do a lot, is harder than it used to be. The human body is designed for all its systems to integrate seamlessly. Each muscle system is balanced against the others. Some of the muscle systems no longer quite do this in my body. Some are no longer completely integrated with the others. They are drummers marching to their own tune, not totally interested in what the rest of me is doing. Movement under those circumstances takes more effort. That's the way it is. I can complain about it or work with it. In order to accomplish this greater effort, I need to stay in shape. When I get the flu or make myself busy with something else and don't get around to exercising, the difference in my gait becomes quite obvious even today. The systems that don't work fluidly will backslide, and I'll again find myself developing compensations that aren't helping me heal. It's up to me to keep training past the disability if I want to be as well and full of life as I can.

My ongoing discipline doesn't take up all my time. I don't spend hours and hours doing my exercises every day. I try to do something most days, however — exercises on the floor, a walk, a trip to the gym to ride the exercise bike, ch'i kung, something. It makes a difference.

## EXPECT THAT PROGRESS WILL BE UNEVEN

We humans like a sure thing. We want to know when we start something that it will move in a straightforward fashion toward the goal we set. In my life I've found this largely to be an illusion. As much as I might cherish the notion of straight-line progress in other parts of my life, I couldn't avoid the reality that it didn't apply to stroke recovery.

I'd assumed that when I began to get better, I'd simply get better and better and better, and that would be that. But that's not how it works. Recovery is episodic. The disability ebbs and flows. It's fascinating. Some days are better than others.

At times I might be able to discern some logical explanation to comfort myself with — maybe I was catching a cold or someone had told me something very sad and I was feeling unmotivated — but most of the time there seemed to be no rhyme nor reason for it.

Some days I would wake up in the morning and the ability I was developing to stand unsupported on my left leg, if only for a few seconds, would be gone. I couldn't keep my balance. Or I'd get out of bed and my left calf would be particularly spastic. Or my speech would be more slurred. Other days I'd wake up and I'd be able to do all the things I'd done the day before and more.

Sometimes the slumps would last for several days before they changed. It was scary. My first thought was typically "I'm getting worse," or "I did something wrong," or "I'll never get anywhere." I had to learn that recovery is simply like this: Some days are better than others. Seven years later, that's still true. Some days I get out of bed and feel very uncoordinated. My left foot slaps on the floor or slides. My hands drop things. Some days the remaining challenges I have recede.

At the beginning, I would become very discouraged by the downturns. I was back to holding on to outcomes, setting myself up by not being willing to simply show up and be with whatever was happening. If I insisted that steady, even progress was a measure of success, and without it I was not succeeding, I was teaching myself to give up the effort and feel sorry for myself. If I could accept that whatever was happening on a given day was only what was happening on that day and not some rigid measurement of good or bad, I could develop some patience and some willingness to be open to what was possible.

Getting discouraged and giving up is the absolute enemy of recovery. Do that, and nothing much happens. I found that when I was patient and worked through the downturns, my long-term movement was toward wellness and improved function.

It's also true that external circumstances have an impact on the quality of function for all of us poststroke. When I'm tired or sick or hurt or cold or several of these at once, I have more trouble walking. My friend Rita has more trouble speaking. My therapist friend Carol has a tremor in her left hand and arm. That's the way it is, and it requires learning and paying attention to the next set of lessons.

PART FIVE

# PRACTICING
# SELF-CARE

# CHAPTER EIGHTEEN

## *You Are the Tool*

PRACTICING SELF-CARE seems as if it would be the easiest lesson to get, but actually it was one of the hardest for me to learn. I'd been trying to learn the art of self-care for years before the strokes. Bob started teaching me about self-care the moment we came together. Sitting in his recliner, he'd watch me pace up and down across the big open room that was the living room, great room, dining room, haven, and center of our home. He'd look at me as I'd talk about this project and that plan and this activity, stretching myself as far as I could, and he would just smile, waiting for me to settle, to come and sit with him, to hold his hand and watch the powerful birds soaring on the air currents in the canyon in front of the windows. When I finally settled, he'd talk quietly with me and share his stories — the things he'd learned from all his experience — and he'd teach me about self-care.

There's a big difference between self-indulgence and self-care. Our society is full to the brim and running over with messages of self-indulgence. We live in a veritable din of words and images suggesting that if only we ate this food, or went on this luxurious trip, or wore this expensive piece of clothing, our lives would be worry free.

Shoving stuff and experiences at ourselves is not self-care. This is evidence of a belief that if we distract ourselves with something exciting enough, life won't happen to us. This is fear covered up by self-indulgence. It can create a kind of addiction.

And here's an interesting thought. Excessive self-restraint or self-sacrifice is often another kind of self-indulgence. It sounds counterintuitive, but if you think about it, it's not. If I sacrifice myself for you, I can tell myself a rich story about how noble or important I am for giving up so much. I talk and act as if I don't matter. Doing this, I can try to make you feel guilty and offload onto you the responsibility for coping with my unwillingness to take care of myself. You owe me since I sacrificed for you. Or if I sacrifice myself out of fear, I might be refusing to face the fear and take responsibility for changing my life rather than staying a victim. Either way, I'm preoccupied with myself or, as we commonly say, I'm being selfish.

Self-care starts with a different understanding, one that isn't selfish. Self-care starts with a realization that we're part of a larger whole — that none of us exists independently of one another and everything else. Self-care requires us to take responsibility for ourselves and our relationship to the world around us. We, each one of us, are the parts that form the whole. If I care for the whole, I must care for myself. If I care for myself, I automatically care for the whole. Self-care starts with an open heart and a deep and abiding love for what is, including ourselves. Seems simple, but in fact it's not, and I had a hard time learning it.

My particular form of self-indulgence fell into the self-sacrifice approach to life. The example I grew up with was to learn to put myself down the list when it came to priorities, and to equate love with caretaking. I take care of you and put you first, and that means I love you. If I work too hard and never take a vacation, that means I love you all the better. I didn't seem to have a clue about the impact of what I was doing on myself.

Bob was too wise for this approach to life. Bob knew a lot and, to my everlasting gratitude, taught me a lot. The first of many lessons of self-care that he taught me came in these words: "You can never really love someone else unless you learn to love yourself first." That was something to think about. He wasn't talking about abstract love. He was talking about his loving me and my loving him.

As I was growing up, I'd often heard the principle "Love your neighbor as you love yourself." I'd always experienced these words as a call to empathy, but I'd never thought about the fact that in order to love my neighbor well, I had to first love myself well. What did it mean to love myself and practice self-care?

Yetta Bernhard, the wonderful woman who taught me about living around limitations, paid a lot of attention to self-care and wrote books about it. Bob not only introduced me to Yetta; he also gave me her books to read. I read them. I thought about what she wrote and what Bob said. I looked around me. Most folks I knew didn't seem to know much more about self-care than I did, except Bob. I watched him. Bob was good at it. He never pushed himself too hard. He enjoyed his life. He knew his limits. He made commitments he could keep. He was good at saying no and saying yes. He was very kind to himself. I never saw him treat himself badly. I understood that I could relax and trust him to speak up for himself and take care of himself. I was impressed.

One day as I was driving home, near the turn up the mountain — in a hurry, impatient, and no doubt failing to pay enough attention to how I was driving — I had the dawning of an insight. As I thought about my lack of regard for my own well-being as I cheerfully threw myself into one project after another, I realized that what I did had a direct impact on Bob. I finally saw that I needed to take care of myself. If I got in an accident or worked so hard I made myself sick, my hurt would hurt Bob. If I were hurt, I would take his energy, and I'd cause him the pain of seeing me in trouble. I began to understand that if I truly loved Bob, and I surely did, the more I took care of myself, the more comfort and ease I would give him. "Aha!" I thought. "I'm really getting this."

And I *was* getting it, to some extent. At least I was seeing half of the lesson — how taking care of myself was taking care of Bob — but it took my strokes to drive the rest of the lesson home. Sitting in my wheelchair looking across the gym at the water fountain I couldn't operate with one hand, I knew I was faced with the task of my own stroke recovery and the words "Nobody knows. It depends on . . . you." I was learning that the most important tool I had for my recovery or for any other aspect of my own life was myself — my brain, my body, me. Many people could help me — wonderful, amazing people. And they did help me. I would never say I did it alone. But the major tool I had to work with was me.

I could either treat that tool well or treat it badly. I could either love that tool and have some care and compassion for it, or I could use it with little concern for its long-term well-being. When I used my really good paintbrush, the one I'd worked to buy, I wouldn't smash it against the paper as I painted and then leave it squashed down and covered with paint. A great watercolor paintbrush is agile and responsive. When I have one, I respect it and enjoy its subtle flexibility as I paint. Then I carefully wash it and put it away to dry. If I had a really good garden tool, I wouldn't break rocks with it and then leave it outside all winter. I'd take care of it. I would understand that it would only remain truly useful if it were taken care of. I was no different from the paintbrush or the garden tool. I was the tool to fashion my life with, and I needed to be careful of and caring toward myself.

This was a big lesson. Maybe having so little energy and resilience to waste poststroke finally made this clear to me. I really couldn't afford to fool myself. I had no margin for error. I had to understand that if I was going to do anything well, I'd better be thoughtful about how I was using myself.

This was a very important insight. My friend Betty Joan tells me that people with brain injuries have a tendency to take less care of themselves than those without brain injuries. I would need to intentionally work at practicing self-care.

How did that understanding translate to action? What could I do?

## BE SAFE

The first and foremost thing to learn in self-care, particularly in stroke recovery, is to stay safe. This lesson wasn't easy for me. I had the impulse-control problem I've described earlier — wanting to get way ahead of myself — and I was so awkward, so unsteady, and in many ways so unpredictable physically. I couldn't depend on my body to do the same thing the same way each time. Sometimes my parts would go more or less where I told them, and sometimes they wouldn't. Random variations appeared.

The brain reacts to injury in a predictable way. My friend and mentor Stanley Keleman tells me that spasticity is a way for the body to hold its shape. If the response to injury were that my muscles had gone flaccid, rather than stiff, I would have fallen over. There would have been no standing up and trying to walk. I could walk if my leg was stiff and wooden, even if the walking was ungainly and not smooth, but I couldn't walk if the muscles of my leg had gone slack in response to the injury.

So the brain, in fear for its life, tightened my muscles into unresponsive spasticity. My job was to reforge the communication between my brain and muscles, and to let my brain know that it was safe to let the muscles relax normally. My brain had been injured and was wary of further insults to the body as it tried to find a way to live with what had happened. If I injured myself, my brain would react with more, not less, spasticity. That's what happens.

Any injury, no matter how small — even an ingrown toenail, as Erwin used to say — would result in more spasticity.

That's a big problem. One of the enormous benefits of early rehabilitation is the message the work sends to the brain that it's okay to let go of the spasticity, or *tone*, as the therapists call it. If the spasticity becomes too ingrained, it's very hard to work it out. The last thing you want to do is increase it.

I had to learn to do everything safely and to manage my impulse control. The house was a challenge. The mountain was a challenge. There were endless opportunities for me to hurt myself. I was trying to cook. I was cutting things in the kitchen. My right hand was improving, but it was still unsteady, and my left hand was quite unpredictable. I couldn't afford to let the knife slip and cut me. I couldn't afford to let the hot water in the pot splash on me and burn me. I couldn't afford to fall on the stairs or when I got in and out of the shower.

To move required me to think about what I was doing and to have a strategy for how to do it. Going down that curved staircase to take a shower took a campaign. How would I grasp the rope railing? The rope was on the left. My left side had little coordination and no strength. How would I hold on to the pole that ran down the other side and grasp the ends of the wooden steps that stuck out on the way down? How would I get from the bottom of the staircase to the bathroom? Carrying a cane down the stairs was unsafe, so I got a second cane and had an upstairs cane and a downstairs cane, each stored at the edge of the stairs.

Once in the bathroom, I sat on the chair I had asked Jacob to put along the wall across from the sink. It was much safer for me to sit on a chair to take off my clothes than to try to undress standing up. We put a bench to sit on in the shower. Standing was both slippery and unsafe and would tire me too much at first. I'd carefully slide the shower door open, step over the rim, and lower myself to the bench. Jacob put a nozzle on a hose so I could sit and wash myself, and a bar in the shower and on the counter just outside the shower so there would always be something to hold on to if my legs were weak. Where did I put the shampoo and the soap so I could easily reach them without losing my unsteady balance on the stool? Every part of the shower had to be thought out before I started.

For a time at home, I needed help. While Bob was amazingly strong, he knew that at his age he was not the best candidate to help me, so we invited a family member to come live with us for my first two weeks back home. After he left, a friend came a couple of days a week to do things for me that I couldn't do myself. Complete honesty about my capabilities was necessary. No room for embarrassment or self-deception here. I dared not force myself to do the things I wasn't ready to do. The opportunity for injury was simply too great.

Even years later, the potential for an increase in spasticity in response to an injury doesn't completely disappear, or at least it hasn't in my case. Rita and I have both had falls in the last couple of years that resulted in a broken bone in our right hands. I fell walking on the mountain. She fell walking in the hills. Neither of us are in the early stages of our recoveries where avoiding injuries is so critical, but for both of us there was an uptick in spasticity while we healed. Rita also experienced an uptick in speech problems, and I experienced more challenges with the emotional affect disorder. Our brains are confident enough now that the problems have passed. But thank goodness this didn't happen to either of us in the beginning, when it was vitally important to take every precaution not to get hurt.

## HAVE FUN

Strokes tend to make people serious. We think, "This is a tragedy. I have to be solemn." Just as it's important not to forget to laugh, we're better off if we don't forget to have fun. How do children learn coordination? They play. They don't get serious and march around with long faces. We delight in watching kittens and puppies and young mammals of all kinds running and jumping in joyous enthusiasm. Play is how mammals develop physical skills. Fun and coordination are interdependent. When we invest too much seriousness in the process of therapy and recovery, we miss a big part of what's life-giving and important.

During my recovery, I'd make sure to be outside some of the time, tossing balls, relearning hopscotch, taking walks on the mountain in the evening when the sunsets created stunning 360-degree panoramas of color, playing games with my grandsons, having fun. Rita plays in her kitchen cooking, delighting in the game of making wonderful food. She wouldn't do it if she didn't have such a good time.

Fun and coordination build upon each other. It's vital for people to have fun. Particularly when they've had strokes. If we get miserable, we focus on our losses and we swim in seriousness. We can give up the seriousness and go swimming in the pool. Splash in the water. Play board games. Go to the beach. Be inventive. Whatever you do, have fun. Having fun will bring life back into the body and help you relearn coordination. It will help you find the pleasure in your own life, just as it is. And, as I was to discover, it would help me minimize the stresses that could so easily arise in my recovery.

# CHAPTER NINETEEN

## *Minimizing Stressors*

THERE ARE MANY KINDS OF INJURIES. Before I learned the lessons of self-care, I knew that a burn or a cut or a broken bone was clearly an injury. What I wasn't so clear about is other ways I might be injuring myself. When did challenges turn into stresses? Sitting around and not pushing the edge of my recovery clearly wasn't productive. But I found that pushing myself too far wasn't productive either. I needed to find a balance.

## REST

I was so tired and had so little energy at the very time I needed to work hard. Fatigue interferes with everything. When I was too tired, I became unfocused and potentially careless. I couldn't hold the concentration and pay close enough attention to what I was doing. If just making a sandwich was a major aerobic event, what could I do?

I learned to rest in between everything. As hard as I'd worked in rehab, I only had my exercises to do. Others fed me, washed my clothes, made my bed, gave me a shower, paid the bills, and determined my schedule, which allowed me to concentrate on my appointments with my therapists.

Now that I was home and turning everything into an opportunity for therapy, I had to rethink what I was doing. I couldn't work in the way I was used to working when all I had to do was go to my appointments. Now I had to pace myself much more carefully than I had in rehab. For someone who was used to expending herself carelessly with little attention on the energy reserve I had left, this was quite a new discipline to learn.

Bob was my teacher in this too. Bob never did anything to the point of overdrawing his energy reserve; he never even got close to empty. I never once saw him overtired. He stopped and rested when he needed to. I thought about this and realized that Bob's approach to managing his energy was symbolized in the way he dealt with the gas tank of his car. Bob never let the gas tank get lower than half-empty. Before my strokes, I'd complain about having to go to the gas station more often than seemed necessary to me. I'd frequently let my tank run down to the point where the little gas station symbol lit up to tell me I'd better do something quickly. Then I'd inevitably have to undertake a desperate search for a gas station at the very moment I was hurrying to get someplace I was already late for. After my strokes, I saw that keeping my gas tank half-full meant I never had to worry if I were faced with an emergency. I always had enough. The idea was always to keep enough of a reserve of whatever energy I needed. "Oh," I thought. "That's how it works — keep a reserve and always have enough." Applying this principle to my own energy was a novel idea.

And so I learned to rest. I sat down and waited between efforts until I had plenty of strength to try the next thing. I took naps. I went to bed early. This made my work more efficient and effective, and helped me build stamina, which then allowed me to work harder. Resting when I needed to didn't result in my sitting around and doing nothing. Resting resulted in better work and, fairly quickly, more work. I wasn't wasting time and energy struggling. I was working with enough gas in the tank.

Sitting down and resting brought some unexpected benefits. One day when Bob and I were sitting in the kitchen resting, I turned and looked out the window by the stove. Our house, like many on the mountain, is set into the side of a hill with the back at or below ground level and the front in the air. It sits nestled into the hill, and the window by the stove, with its curved wooden border, has an intimate view at eye level onto a path that wends its way up to the side of the ridge. It's like looking out at a giant terrarium, seeing a secret life displayed in front of us. As I turned, perfectly framed in the window were two deer, a doe and a fawn, standing on the path. While Bob and I watched, the deer touched noses in the most tender and vulnerable way as if they were kissing — sharing a private moment of affection, completely oblivious to the wonderment of the people safely inside the house.

My friend Rita makes it clear to the patients we talk with that she too still pays close attention to getting enough rest. When Rita takes a long hike, she comes home and takes a nap. She's wise to do this. When I forget this lesson, which I sometimes do now that I have more energy, I regret it. Then I think of Bob and use his practice of keeping his gas tank at least

half-full as a reminder of his wise approach to energy management. Keeping enough energy in reserve invariably allows
me to do more than I'm able to do when I use myself up. It
sounds like a contradiction, but it works.

"Rest in the heart of peace," Buddhist teacher Jack Kornfield likes to say. "Find a place to rest in the middle of things,"
Zen Hospice founder Frank Ostaseski counsels. The two
practices are different sides of the same coin. As I worked
with resting and not pushing myself past my abilities, I realized a simple truth: If I had a peaceful, heart, I could rest anywhere, and if my heart was not peaceful, I could never rest.

If you effort yourself past your inner peace, you don't succeed in accomplishing anything.

## EMOTIONAL UPSET AND WORRY

So many emotions arise during recovery. We need to find a
way to work with them without adding unnecessary stress.
Anger is an ongoing part of recovery. Loss and frustration
and grief inevitably bring some anger along with them. I was
angry that I'd lost so much. I was angry that I had to work so
hard. I was angry that I couldn't do more. Anger is part of
the emotional soup. If we work with it skillfully, the thrum-
ming fire in the blood that anger brings can help to motivate
us to make the effort we need to heal.

It isn't necessary or helpful, however, to stir the anger
up and dwell on it or act out because of it. I could easily
have picked a fight with Bob to deal with my pent-up anger
and created an argument as a diversion from thinking about
my own concerns. But taking my anger out on him would

ultimately have made me feel worse, and it would have stirred up the emotional tension in the house, adding to my stress. Fortunately for me, picking a fight with Bob was not something you did lightly. With his experience and training, you couldn't outthink him and you couldn't outwait him.

I needed to work with my emotions and experience them, but I certainly didn't need to stir up emotional storms in the house, and I didn't need to add to the stress I was already dealing with by hurting the people around me or trying to put responsibility on anyone else for what was happening in my life.

Bob had a great technique for dealing with anger. He would hunch down, tense all his muscles, and growl. That way he released his anger and didn't let it get in his way. I wasn't quite so skillful in my anger release. One day I got really mad and kicked the bathroom cabinet under the sink, and Jacob had to come and fix the latch. But even that was better than increasing the emotional stress by lashing out at someone or holding on to and nursing my anger.

After a stroke or any other major health event, so much has changed, which often causes us emotional distress and worry. We worry whether we'll get well. We worry whether we'll be able to work again. I worried whether Bob was taking proper care of himself. I worried what my grandchildren would think when they finally saw me. I worried that I might never paint again. There were plenty of things to worry about, but there always are, if we look for them.

It's easy to spend a lot of time worrying about things that might happen. Worry — focusing on fears of the future, nursing and holding on to upsetting emotions — leads to emotional unease. There were so many ways to stir the emotional pot and increase my worry and distress, but none of that would help me. I already faced more than enough emotions to work with. Adding unnecessary emotional tension was and is a stressor. Stressors increase spasticity and break concentration. I couldn't afford to do that to myself. Staying present and calm and cheerful as much as I could was much more useful.

I had enough to deal with facing what was happening right in the present moment. What I might or might not be able to do someday in the future wasn't happening right then. My job was to concentrate on what I could do, not what I might or might not be able to do.

What was happening in the present moment was seeing how carefully I could do the bridging exercises, or figuring out how to wash dishes with one hand barely working. That was what was happening. I couldn't know if my hand would get better. I could only find out by maximizing my efforts in the present moment to work with what I had. Like the "Why me?" question I talked about earlier, worry drew me away from what was real and wasted energy on something that didn't exist. I didn't want to use my slowly accumulating energy reserves on something that unproductive.

Easier said than done, you say. And it is. One of the gifts of most spiritual practices is the learning about acceptance. The spiritual paths I'm most familiar with teach a kind of humility, an acceptance of what is. Acceptance is not passive. It's not saying, "Oh, the world and my life are terrible.

There's no point in doing anything." Acceptance is a radical act that requires real courage. Acceptance is the beginning of hope. Acceptance of what is — working with things just as they are — provides the foundation for wise and focused action.

Once I got home and was facing the day-to-day reminders of my life, it took work to avoid distracting myself and wasting energy on worry about the future. I'd learned to stay focused in rehab, but being in rehab was far removed from an ordinary life. Then I was so desperate that staying focused was in many ways easier. Now I was in my own environment and making progress. Now I had a little more energy. Now I had more freedom and more energy to worry. But it still didn't help to use myself that way, and my challenge was to continue to accept my life just as it was.

Continuing to develop the skill to be with what is and to explore what is unfolding, avoiding side excursions into stress and worry, comes with practice, like all other learning. When I began to distract myself with worry, I could practice. Any small, focused act, such as washing dishes, could be used as a way to stay present with what was happening. Washing dishes, letting go of worry about whether or not my dish washing would ever be "perfect" and simply seeing what I could do with any given dish, was a practice.

Stirring the emotional pot or lashing out to vent feelings is not the same thing as a healthy processing of emotions. One causes stress and wastes energy. The other — feeling emotions as they arise, greeting them with loving acceptance, and giving ourselves the time to work through them — allows release and space in our spirits so that we can begin again to work with what is happening in the present moment.

I found that grieving was ongoing. I remember one morning in particular. I got up, sat in the big green chair with our cat Sam and a blanket on my lap, and cried and cried and cried, tears streaming down my face. The ostensible trigger was some building my neighbor was doing, but that wasn't really the issue. The construction was a nuisance but not a major problem. Rather, tiredness, frustration, fear, and grief were rising up in me and had to be given space. This need to cry and cry happened many times, and sometimes the emotions felt overwhelming, but when I gave them space they passed. The feelings that arise over the course of recovery have to be experienced, not pushed away, so that they can move through like storm clouds and leave clear air in their place.

## EATING WELL

If I'm my own best tool to maximize my chances of recovery and if taking care of the tool is important, then it follows that if I feed myself well, I'll improve the way I function. The brain is trying to heal. What is good brain food? Good brain food is not so different from good food in general — low in cholesterol and sugar, high in fiber, part of a diet with plenty of vegetables, fruits, and grains. The daily news is full of stories about the increasing understanding that what we eat can be one of the most helpful things we can do for our bodies. Of course there are specific foods that are particularly good for the brain: dark leafy greens, berries, foods rich in color, and foods rich in omega-3 oils, including certain kinds of fish and nuts. All of these things may help. We each have our own particular nutritional needs. Learn what's the best nourishment for you and give yourself the gift of it.

I came home from the hospital underweight. I needed to pay attention to what I ate, and when, so I could maximize what little energy I had. I was hungry. I felt happy to be alive and grateful to be hungry and to be able to eat. I remember the day back in Kam's office when I was finally given permission to eat a salad. Salad is one of my all-time favorite foods. As Kam watched, I was so careful to chew up every bite and swallow. I didn't want to fail the test. I was going home and wanted to know that I could eat what my body craved.

Since meal preparation was a challenge at home, it became more necessary than ever that I not waste time and calories on foods that wouldn't help me heal. Simple foods can be very nourishing, and planning and preparing what Bob and I could eat became another creative opportunity. How best could I solve this problem and feel delight in the result?

## STIMULATION

The brain needs stimulation to direct its remapping efforts, but too much stimulation overloads it and creates confusion. How was I to find the right balance? I was learning how to rest, but what about things like music and television and people coming to visit and going out for rides in the car? What was nourishing? What was too much? This was not something I could figure out in advance, and it wasn't something that anybody else could figure out for me.

It seems there was only one way I could learn this, and that was by occasionally going past my limits. My old limits no longer had any relevance, and at first I simply didn't know where a limit was until I ran over it. Then my body would react. I learned after the two-hour board meeting that resulted in two days of exhaustion that I wasn't yet ready for that kind of activity. I learned about watching television and listening to music the same way. At a certain point, my head would hurt and my brain would start to ache — which is a different feeling from a regular headache — and my thinking would get mushy. When that happened, I knew I'd passed a limit. From this experience, I'd get a better idea where I'd best stop the next time.

Eventually I began to notice when I was right on the edge of a limit and it was time to pull back. Before the strokes and the lessons after, I'd been good at "overloading myself," as Bob used to call it. Now becoming mindful of my limits and seeing the hurt I caused was another way to learn the practice of self-care. Until the strokes, I'd never focused enough attention on how I damaged myself with certain behaviors. I was learning not to abuse myself and cause pain, but there was another important side to self-care I was also learning, a lesson about being kind to myself.

# CHAPTER TWENTY

## *Being Kind to Yourself*

D URING MY RECOVERY, I began to think, "What if I extended the practice of lovingkindness to myself? What if I did more than avoid hurt? What if I started being intentionally kind to myself?" All my life, like most people, I had a voice in my head that would criticize me: "You're doing it wrong. Can't you see how stupid this is? Why in the world did you choose that one?" — and on and on and on. I had plenty of opportunity to find things to criticize myself for poststroke. I could do very little, and what little I could do was plenty ungraceful. I, who had prided myself on possessing a certain elegance, a certain finesse, could only watch helplessly as I dropped food all over my shirt when I tried to eat. Getting in and out of the car was a major feat of turning and ducking and sitting and swinging my legs in. Nothing graceful about that.

I was frustrated with my left hand. I could easily sit in my wheelchair and call it names. "Stupid hand!" But what good did that do? Did it help me heal? I don't think so. When babies are learning to walk, do we encourage them by yelling at them and telling them how stupid they are because they're not perfect? No, we delight in the progress they are making and celebrate with them. How was what I was doing different from what babies do in learning to walk? Fundamentally, it wasn't. Babies are learning to coordinate their brains with their muscles. That's what I was doing too. The fact that I'd once known and now didn't was immaterial. What mattered was that I was learning just like a young child. If, in the process, I could also learn to talk kindly and encouragingly to myself, my brain would be more likely to respond.

Judging myself inadequate and telling myself I didn't measure up came from a dictate I'd created about how I was *supposed* to do something. What good was that? Clearly I no longer had the ability to do things in a predetermined way. It wasn't possible. The toes on my left foot wouldn't move no matter how many times I yelled at them and compared them with the way they were *supposed* to work. Criticizing myself was yet one more way to avoid facing the truth — the way it was.

I began to notice the running commentary in my mind and try to shift it to a more positive note. Rather than criticizing myself, I began to make an effort to appreciate the work I was doing and the progress I was making. I was learning to thank my hand for all the times it tried to open, all the times the fingers moved a little more. I was learning to tell it, "Good job!" This wasn't something I was used to; it took practice.

Appreciating my efforts, thinking kind thoughts about myself, led me to think about ways to reward myself for all the good work I was doing. I started to pay attention to the things that gave me comfort. No matter how gently I might talk about the recovery process at times, the truth is that recovery is hard work. Doing nice things for myself lightened my spirits and brought me moments of respite and ease.

There were many small, easy ways to give myself pleasure then, just as there are now. Then maybe it was having some flowers in the house. Maybe it was having a cup of tea from my favorite mug as I sat holding hands with Bob. Now maybe it's eating popcorn. I must confess to a weakness for popcorn — warm and slightly salty, smelling of butter and crunching so noisily in my mouth. Yum!

In whatever ways I could think of, I began to give myself the ease of small kindnesses. These kindnesses lightened my spirits and improved my mood, but they also did something else. They sent a message to my brain that encouraged it to focus on healing. If I acted in a way that valued and respected my body, my brain was reminded to do this too.

My friend Jean is very good at this. She's amazing to watch. Jean was a very talented professional dancer before her stroke. She had a hemorrhage so severe that it required surgery to stop the bleeding, and she was in a coma for three days. Afterward the doctors told her she would never walk again. If anyone knows how to work, it's a dancer. Jean ignored the doctors and worked and worked and worked. Now she walks without a cane. Although her left peripheral vision is gone, she took special drivers-education courses and is now driving again, to her great delight.

When Jean wants to do something, she does it. She decided early on that she wouldn't sacrifice her joy in life just because she had a stroke. With her husband, Jean plans romantic weekend getaways, and travels to Alaska, Hawaii, or wherever feels right. Jean doesn't hesitate to seek out the activities, small and large, that bring pleasure to her life.

## HAVING A COACH

As I was preparing to leave the rehab center, I spoke to Erwin. I knew I was leaving five to six hours per day, five days a week, of therapy plus part of the day on Saturdays, and while I was clear that I'd need to create my own schedule at home, I also knew that I could benefit from more help than I'd be able to get coming back to rehab for two one-hour appointments a week. I was a businessperson who was used to solving problems. I recognized this sudden change in the amount of scheduled work as a problem that needed to be solved. I asked Erwin if he knew of anyone who could work with me at home. I could schedule my work, but I wanted a coach to help me stay focused.

Erwin said he would think about my request. The next day he told me that he did know someone who was a physical therapist, experienced in stroke recovery. She had worked at the rehab center but left because she'd given birth to twins and wanted to stay at home with them. He told me that she occasionally worked with people, and he thought she might be available to help me. Then he told me where she lived. He described a location that turned out to be within walking distance from my house on the mountain! I'm not kidding. I was stunned. Blessings are indeed everywhere.

That's how I came to know Suzanne. I didn't know it until I asked for help, but Suzanne was a huge blessing just waiting to happen. This was another example of what Jacob says: "You find what you look for." I was looking for help, and I was looking for blessings. I got both in the same package.

This blessing named Suzanne told me that when she found out from Erwin how disabled I was when I came home, she wondered if she should meet me at our house. She knew the mountain and how challenging it can be, and was worried that Bob and I wouldn't be able to cope. This sweet concern was simply evidence of the warmth and generosity that are so much a part of Suzanne. I'd never met Suzanne at the various neighborhood functions Bob and I had attended over the years, but it turned out that I already knew her in-laws, who also lived close by. When Erwin told me who Suzanne was, I could barely believe my good fortune. And when I met Suzanne, I was even more grateful. We immediately became fast and loving friends.

Suzanne became my coach. The work of recovery requires a level of focus that's similar in many ways to training for a sport. When we train ourselves for a sport, we don't try to do it on our own. We get a coach. We all need reinforcement, and it's useful to have someone to help us stay on task and meet goals. I was fortunate that my coach knew physical therapy. That was wonderful, but it isn't, by any means, the only way to have a coach. A coach can be a friend, a family member, a professional, or a neighbor — whatever works for you. The point is to have one.

Suzanne came to see me for an hour or two a couple of times a week. She helped me stay focused. I chose to use her as someone I would hold myself accountable to, and she helped me keep my attention where it needed to be. Suzanne, knowing the power of the challenges the mountain sets because she also lives here, got me out on the hiking paths early, in a brace, with a cane, if only for a few steps, just to help me dream of possibilities.

We would invent new exercises or variations on old ones to broaden the creative challenge. One of the exercises I learned as an outpatient after I left the rehabilitation center was crossover walking. I'd step sideways with my right foot, then step my left foot across my right in front, step to the right with the right foot, and then bring the left foot across my right foot in the back. I'd repeat the pattern several times and then do it in the opposite direction with the opposite feet. To help me keep my balance, Suzanne would hold my hands and mirror me with her feet, moving sideways with me to keep me steady. Once I was able to do the exercise in the house on a flat surface, we began to do it sideways up and down the sloped gravel parking area, and eventually up and down the steep street.

Suzanne and I would also play catch together to improve my coordination and quick response, tossing balls back and forth and laughing. Suzanne has a wonderfully joyous sense of fun. Once I was able to walk on trails for more than a few steps, we'd hike them together, starting with short distances and building our way up to longer and longer hikes.

But perhaps even more important than the support of my self-discipline was the way Suzanne could celebrate the small victories with me. I was so engrossed in what I was doing, struggling with each effort, that I'd often fail to notice my incremental progress. Suzanne would say to me, "See how much farther the fingers of your left hand are opening today than they were last week?" The change would be very small, but it would be there, and with Suzanne's support I was able to acknowledge it and appreciate my body for the effort and the success. What that did for my motivation in the daily grind of recovery was beyond price.

Having a coach was so helpful in many ways. One of the other ways was that it kept me from holing up on the mountain and isolating myself. Working with Suzanne, I could see the benefit of being engaged with another person. I became determined not to be isolated, not to hide, so I looked for other ways to stay engaged and be a part of life.

For quite a while at the beginning of my recovery, I was very obviously disabled. When I went out somewhere, people stared at me as people do. I wasn't used to this. It made me uncomfortable. I could have stayed at home and avoided the public scrutiny, but I chose not to. I was trying to find appropriate stimulation and a way to live my life with what I had. If I'd let my dislike of being stared at keep me home, who would be the major loser? Me! So I went to the store. I went to the bank. Bob and I visited friends. I went out. I didn't stay by myself.

Knowing other stroke survivors is another way to prevent isolation. While there are many millions of people who have had a stroke, and although strokes happen to people of all ages, even babies, at the beginning I didn't have any friends my age who had experienced a stroke. At rehab I was given some information about a local stroke group. That's how I met my therapist friend Carol, whom I've described earlier. Carol brought me into her world of friends who are stroke survivors. Talking with her, I came to realize that nobody understands what you're going through as well as someone who has been through something similar. I'm so grateful to Carol for that teaching.

I now have many friends who have had strokes. We talk and share and know one another's experience from the inside out. Carol has an aging parent. I had an aging husband. Carol and I could talk about the challenges of working with our ongoing limitations as we met the responsibilities of caring for an older loved one and cheered each other on. My friend Rita and I reach out to other stroke survivors together, go to the movies together, and go hiking together. Seeing how Rita lives around her limitations, particularly on the mountain trails, inspires me to hike greater distances and improve my endurance to keep up with her. If I don't, she will soon be hiking circles around me.

I read stroke literature and stay current with a couple of national magazines. And I give talks regularly at the rehab center, meeting new survivors, hearing their stories. All of this keeps me connected and grateful, and is part of my gift of kindness to myself.

# CHAPTER TWENTY-ONE

## *Reestablishing the Social Body*

WE TEND TO THINK OF OURSELVES as having only one body — the one defined by the tips of our hands and feet and the top of our heads — but in a very real sense we have another body, and that's our social body. Our social body is the web of relationships and roles we've established for ourselves over the years of our lives. It's the energy exchange and the structures we create with the people around us. We're sustained by this structure. Going to work and spending time with friends energizes us and holds us up. We know ourselves in relationship to those we spend time with. Humans are relational beings. We're designed for it.

When people are as gravely injured as they often are as a result of stroke, their ability to participate in the social body in a meaningful way may suddenly be lost as surely as the ability to move a hand or a foot. We immediately notice the loss of the use of a physical body part, but we may not as quickly notice the loss of the social body.

It can be profoundly disorienting to lose our place in the social body. The effects of it begin to be very apparent once we go home. I was lucky. I didn't have a regular job when I was injured. I was working in the studio and had become accustomed to spending a lot of time by myself. I didn't suddenly lose all my connections to coworkers, but I remember how I felt when I left the active real estate business after I married Bob. Even leaving a job in that way was pretty disorienting at first. I was used to having a cup of coffee with my coworkers and putting energy in together on a common project. Standing by myself was hard and lonely.

Sometimes people react to brain injuries as if the lack of moving a limb, or the spasticity walking, means that we're no longer capable of having meaningful social interactions, and that's often the farthest thing from the truth. As we heal, we and the people around us need to make a deliberate effort to include us in all of the social activities.

When my friend Rita went out in public, her disabilities, her halting speech, her unresponsive right arm, and her impaired walking gait caused people to pull away from her. Sometimes when she was walking, mothers would cross the street to take their children out of her path. This destruction of the social body is extraordinarily isolating. Rita tells the story of walking into the small town center near where she lives, feeling very isolated and sad, and meeting Ron Kovic, who wrote the book *Born on the Fourth of July*. Kovic is a Vietnam veteran who's using a wheelchair due to war injuries. Kovic was immediately drawn to Rita and included her in the conversation, understanding that despite her disabilities she was a person like any other who thrived on social contact. Remembering that day, when she was finally seen as a complete human being despite her obvious disability and was included as a member of a social body, still moves Rita to tears of gratitude.

Another stroke survivor, Randy, was very fortunate. His friends at the office knew he needed them. They called. They came by and discussed work problems with him. As soon as Randy was able, they included him in social activities related to work, inviting him to birthday parties and picnics. They were supporting his social body. One of Randy's aims was to be able to go back to work. His employer had a thoughtful disability policy and began to create a way for Randy to see himself as an ongoing participant in that social body.

After her stroke, another survivor, Barbara, went back to work part-time as soon as she could. She needed time to work on her rehabilitation, and she also needed the interaction that maintained her social body. Barbara lives alone. Being in connection with her work brought her nourishment that she vitally needed.

Sometimes the old social body cannot be reclaimed. Then a new one must be built. Providing that opportunity is a vital support that friends and family can bring. When we're injured, working with friends and family and finding how we can participate in the world as we're healing is a crucial recovery task.

## VALUE YOUR FRIENDS AND YOUR FAMILY

Not being isolated and the gratitude that arises from this blessing provides me with an ongoing reminder that I didn't transform my experience alone. I may have been responsible for being willing to show up and work, I may have been the tool that I used, but my healing was a community effort. As I write this section, my heart wells up. So many people — from my family to the rehab specialists to people walking in the street who were careful of my cane — are a part of my remarkable healing.

My job, which I was quite unprepared for, was to learn how to accept their help. I had always been the helper, not the one helped. Since I'd commingled love and caretaking, I was at a loss to understand why people still liked me when I was incapable of doing anything for them. I was truly perplexed. I didn't know how to communicate effectively from that position of perplexity. I needed to learn how to speak up.

Frustration was my first teacher. Reaching for anything with only one hand functioning, and that one hand shaking, required a major-league effort. Back in rehab, the little tape player was my companion and my comfort, especially late at night. I would strategize and work and work to put it just where I could reach it on the tray table next to my bed — carefully, carefully so that it was not too close to the edge where I'd knock it over and not so far away that I couldn't grasp it. I'd put the tape next to it and get ready to go to sleep. Then the nurse would come in and start tidying up for the night and unconsciously move the tape player and the tape to the dresser, where there was no hope of my reaching it. I had to learn to say, "Please, please, put that back. I had it just where I needed it."

That went okay. I got used to saying when I didn't like something. Now I needed to expand the practice beyond reacting. I would have to start thinking about what would be beneficial and learning to ask for it. Those were harder lessons. I had to ask for something I wanted just because it would bring me comfort. I was cold. Rehab was always cold for me. My blood pressure is low and at night, lying still, I would shiver. I started with Jacob. Asking Jacob felt easier than asking other people. He was with me so often, listening, sharing thoughts, and holding the space with his calm strength. I asked Jacob to bring me a blanket. The results of that request were wonderful. I was never cold at night again, and I slept better.

People wanted to help me. I wasn't doing them any favors by not speaking up and helping them do skillfully what they wanted to do anyway. One night when I was giving a talk and got to this topic, a man whose wife had had a stroke told me that together he and she had come up with a list of things that people could do to help: bring over a meal, take her for an appointment, sit with her when he had to go out, go shopping — all sorts of things. Then when people asked to help, they could look at the list, choose something, and know that what they did was a real benefit.

I'd learned to say when I didn't like something and to ask for what I wanted; now I had to learn to ask people to be patient with me because it was also important that I be able to tell people when *not* to help me. I had to be able to say, "I know you can pick that piece of paper up off the floor a hundred times faster than I can, but I need the practice. Please let me do it myself." It's hard for people who love you to watch you struggle. You have to ask for their tolerance.

## WISE SPEECH

The Buddhists teach *wise speech*, a way of communicating that includes refraining from using words to cause an injury, whether directly, by saying unkind things to someone's face, or indirectly, by saying unkind things about someone who isn't present — in other words, by spreading gossip. It's quite amazing when you think about the amount of injury, hurt feelings, low self-esteem, lack of motivation, and pain that are caused by the way we talk with and about one another. I came to see that communicating my needs to the people around me with kindness and patience was one way to practice wise speech.

I'd learned to say what I wanted and what I didn't want, and to ask for patience and tolerance. I also benefited from being very careful about the way I spoke. How we speak conveys as much or more than the facts we're trying to communicate. The practice of wise speech makes a difference, particularly to the people who are caring for you day in and day out, whose roles are so hard.

The role of a caregiver is really very difficult. A year and a half after my stroke, my beloved husband began to be increasingly unwell. Bob's difficulties resulted in my being his caregiver for the remaining two years of his life. In many ways, recovering from a stroke was easier than being Bob's caregiver. Caregiving requires you to show up and be helpful at the same time you're dealing with your grief and rage that someone you love is suffering. Caregiving thrusts a responsibility into the midst of your life that you may be unprepared for, and you may have little time or resources with which to meet that responsibility.

As stroke survivors, or as survivors of whatever else has befallen us, we have a responsibility to our caregivers as well as to ourselves. Our job is to ask for what we need and make clear what we don't need at the same time we find ways to care for, appreciate, and be patient with our caregivers. They love us. They're doing the best they can with a job that they're not prepared for, in a situation that causes them to struggle with their own emotions.

A little appreciation goes a long way. The entire time I knew him, Bob always said thank-you. He said thank-you for small things and thank-you for big things. One of my favorite thank-yous was the one he said when he went to bed. He would say, "Thank you for another wonderful day." It didn't matter what we had done that day. He was grateful for the day and able to say so.

There was a lot that Bob couldn't easily do to care for me, and certainly a lot that I couldn't do at all. Bob could do some things to help me, but he couldn't be my caregiver. We needed help, so Bonnie came. Bonnie was and is an angel. She came into our lives to do the things I couldn't do, such as drive me to my appointments, type letters for Bob, and carry the laundry up the stairs. She helped us twice a week for a while, and then once a week for a longer while. Her radiant heart filled up the house. She's still in my life as a dear friend, a remarkable cherished gift that arose from what happened.

About five months after my strokes, my brother came to

live next door. I'd wanted so much to know and share time with my brother, and now he moved to the West Coast and chose to be close by. He changed jobs and settled here so that he could do things like carry the groceries and move heavy objects and run errands. He still lives next door and, with Bob gone now, his presence is truly a blessing.

So many people helped in my recovery. So many were part of what was happening in ways large and small. I wanted to recognize them, thank them, and appreciate them, so we decided to have a stroke anniversary party. One year after my strokes, we held a party. Friends came. Family came. Neighbors came. I invited my therapists from rehab, but they couldn't come. Perhaps a good thing, since the affect disorder was still very much a part of my what I was dealing with, and I'm not sure I could have found the breath and composure to speak my wealth of gratitude for them in their combined presence, although I've told them many times since. After everyone had eaten and had something to drink, we invited all the people who were there into a circle around the room. I stood in the center and spoke to each one, one by one, out loud so that everyone else could hear, acknowledging their contribution and my gratitude for it. The neighbor who swept the street was there and the neighbor who had cooked the welcome turkey dinner. The contractor neighbor who had come and put in railings along the paths was there. The architect neighbor who had helped me solve a problem was there. Suzanne was there. Bonnie was there. Betty Joan and her husband were there. My family was there. So many people were there.

By then I'd realized that my healing didn't happen in isolation. As I healed, everyone around me was healing too. As I cared for myself, my well-being helped everyone.

Today I do my best to keep the lesson of self-care fresh in my mind in a world where the messages we receive from all quarters rarely support the practice. There's a Buddhist vow that goes: "May I not harm any living being." These days when I say this vow, I add a few words: "May I not harm myself or any other living being," just as a reminder, so that I don't get busy and forget this particular lesson that Bob and my strokes taught me.

PART SIX

# WHAT NOW?

# CHAPTER TWENTY-TWO

## *Beginnings*

SO WHATEVER HAPPENED to that book I was illustrating? I let it go, and I let it go completely. I gave up my dream. Holding on to that dream would never have allowed me to fully participate in my recovery. Focusing on what I could do, not what I might have done, was my task and my responsibility.

I put it behind me, and stopped holding on to it. When Linda, my publisher, came to see me in rehab, I urged her to find another illustrator quickly. I couldn't see any way that I'd ever be well enough to work on the book again, and I felt very sad for the author, Jan, knowing that the realization of her dream had been halted by my stroke. It was Jan's first book too, and it was important to me that she have an illustrator who could take her words and create the book she dreamed of.

I assumed that Linda was doing exactly that — finding another illustrator for Jan's book — but Linda had a different idea. She liked my particular style of illustration for this book, and she decided to hold the project to see what happened. Months into my recovery, she finally told me this. I love her, but I thought she was nuts.

Time passed. I could do so little. Not only didn't I have the coordination to paint; I also didn't have the strength. Linda waited. Nine months after my strokes, I finally went to the studio to try to work on an illustration. Nine months of rehabilitation work, and I finally found the courage to make an attempt. The fine motor control in my right hand was improving, but I still had a lot of recovery in all areas left to do. In the studio, I could only work twenty minutes at a time, even nine months after the strokes. Twenty minutes, and I'd be done for the day. How was I ever going to get anything painted that way?

What did I have to lose? Show up; focus. I'd already let go of the outcome, so I painted. After six weeks of working twenty minutes a day, I finished an illustration. Six weeks! I didn't know if it was good enough. I had little objectivity. With great trepidation, I invited Linda and Jan over to see what I'd done. I would have to be able to paint in a way that was seamless with other work I'd already completed for the book, in a way that blended in. Could I do it? Had I accomplished painting an illustration that worked with others I'd done?

I watched their faces. I held my breath. They looked at the painting, and then they turned fully toward me and smiled as they said, "Yes! This works! We believe you can finish the book, and we're willing to wait some more and see." Could this be true? Was there really going to be a possibility that I could come through those devastating strokes and fulfill my dream?

Amazed, humbled, grateful, open to the possibility, I went to work. Before my strokes, it would have taken me no more than six days to finish a painting. Now it was taking me six weeks, but as I worked and remembered to watch my limits, practice self-care, and not overtire myself, I began to paint a little faster. I again became immersed in the world of the four bears and their cat and dog. With each illustration my confidence grew a little. Given the kind of book it was, each illustration represented a unique challenge, as I took the bears outside of their house and into the day, as the sun set and the characters returned home to their house and night fell.

One after another, I finished the illustrations. The book unfolded. Finally I was ready to paint the last illustration. I didn't paint the paintings entirely in order. I'd saved one in particular to paint last. The last illustration I painted was a new version of the one I'd been painting when the strokes occurred. I was a little nervous about painting this one. Working on it brought back the days just before the first stroke, as I remembered in my body the signs that the stroke was about to occur — the clumsiness, the stress. Tension and the hope mixed with the paint as the painting developed. Would I indeed finish this painting and the book?

I felt the need to create a symbol of the journey, and so in the painting I put something particularly dear to me. The rhyme for that page in the book is "clocks and blocks." The message is about letting go of schedules, and the cat is smiling as it holds a watch in its paw. The watch I chose to paint is the one that was strapped around the neck of my watchdog. That's my private triumph: the watch now in a painting, so tiny, so finely drawn — the product of eyes that could now focus and a body that could now respond.

The book, *Just for Today*, was published three years after my strokes. No one who hasn't been told can tell which three paintings were painted before the strokes and which were painted after, but now you know which one was painted last. On the cover are the words "Illustrated by Alison Bonds Shapiro."

I had done it. I'd illustrated a book. My dream was a reality.

Was fulfilling that dream, the publishing of the children's book, the end of the story? No, in fact, that was just the beginning of the rest of my life.

In the spring before Bob died, three years after my strokes, I got a phone call from the director of operations at the rehab center, Michelle Camicia. Kaiser Permanente wanted to make a short film about the rehab experience to show to families before their loved ones were transferred into the center. Kaiser had hired a video producer named Paul Shain to do the work, and the director wanted to know if I would be willing to help Paul in some way.

I wasn't sure what I could do, but I'm always eager to help the rehab center in any way I can, so I readily agreed. The day before the filming, Paul called me to talk about what he wanted. He asked me both to interview patients while he filmed them and to tell my story for the camera. I didn't know much about being on camera, but I was willing.

I arranged for a caregiver to be with Bob on the appointed day. That spring was one of the most difficult times of his illness, and I was sleep-deprived and stressed. Getting out of the house for a day was a blessing for me. When the caregiver arrived, I was dressed and ready. Carefully taking the car out of the garage, I drove down the mountain on a day when the world was filled with flowers, up across the bay, through the marshlands that line the north bay, home to the elegant slender-legged cranes posing motionless in the shallow water. Rejoicing in the beauty, I headed for Vallejo, an hour north and east of my house.

When I arrived at the rehab center to meet Paul, I discovered that he had set up the crew in the back of the patient dining room. This room, the front filled with tables and chairs, lies at the opposite end of the long hall from the gym. While I was in my wheelchair, I ate dinner there every night that I couldn't persuade my nurse to let me eat in bed. The back of the room, separated from the dining area by a series of heavy, folding partitions mounted to the ceiling, is used for movie night or bingo or other recreational activities and for meetings.

I walked past the tables and chairs in the front section and into the back of the room behind the partitions. Paul welcomed me and then introduced me to the cameraman and the soundman. I greeted them while trying not to stare at the complicated array of lights, microphones, and cameras. The last time I'd seen that room, it had been full of chairs and patients. Now the room looked full even with the chairs cleared away, but it no longer resembled a hospital meeting room. It looked more like something out of a movie set.

I thought we'd be filming in the gym or in the patients' rooms, but, no, we were filming in the very room where I'd watched the film about stroke recovery that had so frustrated and upset me. Now transformed by the paraphernalia of film production, this was the very room where I'd sworn that I'd somehow find a way to be like the former Miss America who could be seen walking in that film, having recovered from a stroke.

I was plenty happy that I was walking, as I'd vowed I would do, and that I could drive and participate in a project of any kind. "I walked into this room," I thought. "How fantastic!" Then Paul called to me, and I focused my attention on what he wanted. Paul gave me directions for interviewing the patients, then filmed them from behind me over my shoulder. I loved it. Talking with these stroke survivors felt so nourishing and inspiring. I asked them questions to put them at ease, and the fact that they were talking to a former patient helped them overcome any camera shyness and express themselves openly and naturally.

When we were finished with the patients, Paul turned the camera on me, and I spoke while the chief of physical and rehabilitation medicine, Dr. Elizabeth Sandel, asked me questions. It was so easy to respond to her. My respect for who she is and what she does is enormous. Absorbed in talking with her, I too barely noticed the camera.

It was a great and satisfying day. The next day at home, musing on the experience, all of a sudden, I realized that I'd not only achieved being like the former Miss America in learning to walk again but to my complete astonishment I had become, in a very real way, the person she was — a person who had been filmed demonstrating my stroke recovery, a symbol of hope. And that filming had taken place in the very room where I'd been so unable to manage my emotional affect disorder while watching the film with the former Miss America in it — the very room in which I'd made the vow to walk again. I was stunned.

This was a blessing beyond anything I could have imagined. Knowing how profoundly disabled I'd been, realizing that I'd survived and recovered and was now going to be in a film about rehabilitation, evidenced the unfolding of a possibility outside my comprehension. I was filled with gratitude and wonder.

But Paul wasn't done with me yet. Later that year, in the summer, with the richness of the experience of talking with patients during filming fresh in my mind, I asked Kaiser Permanente if I might have an opportunity to talk with patients on a regular basis, showing them that recovery was possible, and telling them some of the lessons that had helped me. Kaiser Permanente agreed, and I began to teach.

After I'd been teaching for a while, Paul came to talk with me. As we sat in the cafeteria downstairs in the hospital having tea before the class, Paul looked at me and said, "We should make a film about stroke recovery together." I couldn't believe what I was hearing. Me make a film about stroke recovery? What a preposterous idea!

But Paul was persuasive, and I began to catch the magic of his vision. Knowing what I now knew — that so much of recovery is a result of how we bring ourselves to it, that so much is possible if we're willing to risk finding out — I wanted to make sure that other people got this message early in the process. When I teach at the rehab center, time and time again patients and family members say that learning how much is possible inspires them to try. I saw from Paul the potential usefulness to patients of a simple film on DVD. Patients could have something to watch long before they had the strength to sit up through a one-hour lecture. Given my emotional affect disorder poststroke, I certainly couldn't have sat through an hour-long public presentation while I was in rehab. I would have been completely unable to manage my emotional response. I needed the information, but I would have had a hard time accessing it.

So Paul persuaded me to commit to this project, and we're doing it. We've raised a little money, and we've completed filming. We're making a short DVD that we hope will inspire people to believe in their own potential for recovery. I know how much I could have used a DVD like that when I was first injured. I want other people to have what I didn't have.

# CHAPTER TWENTY-THREE

## *Putting the Lessons into Practice*

IT WAS REMARKABLE THAT I DIDN'T DIE as a result of the two bleeds in my brain stem. As Betty Joan told me months after my strokes, the bleeds were in two different areas, and nearly everything that could have been affected was. My chances for survival were no more than even. My chances for the kind of recovery I've made were considered to be far less.

The lessons of my strokes are engraved on my body as if a bolt of lightning had entered at the back of my head and run across my face, down through my left side, down my chest and groin, down the inside of my leg, and out my foot. The reverberations of the lightning set off the right side and moved things out of balance. This lightning, these strokes, have changed me irrevocably and created a mark that will be there forever.

I was profoundly disabled by the strokes. I'm still partially disabled. But being *disabled* doesn't mean that I'm *unable*. It means that my body is permanently different from those who haven't had a similar experience. I'm reclassed, in a sense, but this reclassification brings with it a blessing. I've learned not to waste my time pushing against what isn't possible, but instead to move directly toward opening to what *is* possible. This is a powerful teaching. My choice is to find a way to live within the constraints of what's true right now about my life, and to act from my center with a peaceful heart — speaking aloud the truth of what I can and cannot do.

My strokes happened. I healed, and now it is my privilege to live out the lessons I've learned from them. These lessons led me through transformation. I've lived it. I know in my very bones that transformation of any situation is possible. This understanding is both humbling and empowering. And with it comes an obligation that I do something with the learning.

I'm still me, with all my scrappiness and all my competitiveness and all my goofiness — a little older, and a little more experienced. I'm simply a person who has had the privilege of living through some extraordinary lessons. I remain all the things that are a package that life carves into the shape called *Alison*. That's not going to go away because I had a stroke.

But I can keep working, and in some senses I'm compelled to keep working, with what I've learned. I can keep putting the lessons into practice.

I began teaching at the rehab center before Bob died, and I knew that Paul and I would someday find a way to make the DVD, but at the time I was doing little else besides taking care of Bob. By the last summer of Bob's life, I was worn-out with years of recovering from a stroke and then taking care of him. After Bob died, I was tired and thought a nice, peaceful, quiet life would be great. I planned to move off the mountain and make my life simple, but that would take a while. There was a lot to sort through and organize before I could go anywhere.

While I was organizing and was still on the mountain without Bob, I thought the best thing I could do was to find a way to be useful to other people. So that's what I wished for — the opportunity to be useful.

As Bob would often say to me, half jokingly and half seriously, "Be careful what you wish for. You might get it."

"Oh, she wants to be useful," life said, and promptly set about opening possibilities. Bob died in October of 2005. In June of 2005, the summer of the year Bob died, my tiredness was deep. I could barely keep up with caregiving responsibilities for both Bob and me. My sense of the future was limited. But in June 2006, there I was: the incoming Chair of the Board of Trustees of Saybrook Graduate School and Research Center, standing on a dais, handing out diplomas at graduation to amazing people who had earned master's and doctorate degrees.

How did that happen?

It happened because recovering from the stroke had taught me much more that I realized. Unconsciously I'd begun to apply the lessons of transformation to the rest of my life. I had no inkling this was true at first, but other people did.

Emerging from the house for the first time after Bob died, in January 2006 I attended a board of trustees meeting of an organization I have helped. I went to the meeting to get out of the house, to be around people for a while, and to observe. I sat quietly while others talked, listening to the dialogue, watching, and occasionally commenting on what I heard.

During the meeting, a request for someone to lead a negotiating team to explore a possibility the organization was

considering was put on the table and discussed. I listened. I
wondered who would do the work. I thought to myself, "Is it
possible they will ask me?" My consulting skills felt a bit rusty
to me after several years of stroke recovery and caregiving,
but I knew that basic skills don't disappear. Reading a balance
sheet is rather like riding a bicycle — not something you easily forget.

Maybe they would ask me. It seemed like a possibility, so
I thought about the situation quite a while in case they did.
What would I do? I was just beginning to surface after an
intense period of mourning, and I wondered what my response would be if I were asked. Would I be able to do it?
Would I want to? I wasn't sure. Since I didn't know what my
life would be like now that Bob had died, I considered the idea
— more as a kind of practice of thinking about my future than
anything else.

I took a walk on the mountain and let the thoughts move
through my mind unobstructed, talking with Bob in my heart,
as I often do now. I wanted to be useful — at least that's what
I'd said to myself, what I'd wished for. Perhaps this or something like it was an opportunity to be useful. "Maybe," I
thought, "I'll consider it if they ask me."

A few days after the meeting, I received a call. Would I
lead the negotiating team? Still unsure, I cautiously agreed. I
wasn't certain why they had asked me. What I hadn't yet realized was that the stroke had changed more than the way I
walk, and other people were eager to put what I'd learned
to use.

The stated request involved performing a negotiation, but

as I was to find out, that wasn't really what the organization needed. The organization was experiencing difficulty, facing a challenge, holding on to a particular outcome. What they needed was transformation. I was chosen for the role because they saw in me something that they were looking for.

On the trip down to a meeting in Southern California, I was quite conscious that my gait is different from other people's, and my pace is slower. I realized how much careful attention I need to pay to the way I walk. I certainly didn't want to fall. But I was also conscious that I was much less impressed by surroundings and titles than I used to be. I was only interested in learning what the situation was — exactly as it was — and opening to the possibilities inherent within it. My patience with pretense, my willingness to play games, had disappeared. I realized that I no longer had anything to prove.

Three of us spent a day in a series of meetings to assess the negotiation process and began to look at the facts and the people involved. Holding the experience positively, with our hearts open, seeing it just as it was, we opened to possibilities. Paying close attention to what we saw, we carefully observed how the results of this negotiation might affect the organization, both positively and negatively.

We took our observations back with us to the organization. Dealing with what was, without adornment or judgment, without grasping or pushing any part of it away — and looking at how it might be worked with, rather than focusing on the perceived limits — began to challenge the organization's preconceived notions of what the future had to look like. The results have been astonishing. The organization has now found its heart, and its future is unfolding in unimagined ways.

"Hmm," I thought. "This looks similar to the process of transformation that I experienced in the stroke recovery. Is there a parallel?"

Then a couple of former clients came back to talk to me to see if I might be open to helping them in their lives and businesses. More answers to my wish to be useful were arising. Was I ready for this? Why not? I had no idea where I'd end up, but recovery had taught me to work and be willing to wait to discover what might happen.

Now I began to look at what I'd learned. I'd had the experience of watching the transformation beginning in the organization I've described working with, and I saw the parallels. What I'd learned in stroke recovery had clear applications in business and personal coaching, and in all the things I was doing. The way I worked had changed fundamentally. My technical skills were no longer the most important tools in my toolbox. They were only truly useful when I employed them in service of the skills of transformation that the stroke had taught me.

Gaining confidence, I deliberately began to apply what I'd learned. My former clients, a husband-and-wife team running a construction company, were at a crossroads in the development of their business. The company was underfinanced and growing very rapidly. We worked together for months — stabilizing, managing, supporting possibilities — once again dealing with the issues just as they were, creating solutions.

Out of this work, the opportunity arose to sell the company at a handsome profit and realize the owners' dreams.

Then I was approached by another set of potential clients. This couple's need was more personal: figuring out how to approach end-of-life care. This was an entirely different kind of issue, but even though the outcome would be the death of one of them, it contained within it the seeds of possibility. How they worked with the challenges arising from illness and dying, how they opened their hearts to the richness of connection, focusing on the possibilities, not on the problems, created a way to live through the passage with grace and love and rich memories of tenderness.

I was standing beside my clients, lending my skills and offering coaching. They were building their own transformations. These were not my creations. My clients were opening to their own unique possibilities as they moved through the issues, challenges, and problems of their lives. What I was doing was providing a bridge for my clients to help them find their way to the changes that would nourish them.

## BRIDGING

During the course of my recovery, I discovered that there's more than one kind of bridging. I'd learned to do one kind of bridging in mats class. That kind stabilized my trunk muscles. There is a very different kind of bridging — one we do to stabilize one another.

When Erwin got me on my feet and stood behind me, not touching me while urging me to take one step and then another, he was doing more than directing me, more than staying close by to right me if I began to fall; he was bridging me from one state of ability to another. By lending me his confidence and his presence, he was giving me the energy to do more than I could have done or would have done on my own.

Jacob came to the hospital to pick me up, and then he stayed at home with Bob and me during my first twenty-four-hour home visit from rehab. He was there, on call, with his big, loving, gentle strength, spending the night on a couch way too small for his tall body. He made himself available for any need that might arise. He could even pick me up and carry me if I found I couldn't manage. The security of Jacob's presence gave me strength to face the enormous challenges the house represented. He didn't do things for me that I could do for myself, but by standing beside me, he allowed me to reach farther and accomplish more than I would try alone. His loving help is another example of bridging. I was borrowing his strength to learn my own.

In Marin County, where I live, the rains come in the winter. Summer is generally dry, brown, sere. Winter is full of water. The mountain has few natural springs and no ponds, so when the rains come the water races off the hills down to the sea. We have glorious, tumbling waterfalls in the winter where only bare rocks exist in the summer.

One winter day when we had a break in the rains, my wonderful coach Suzanne suggested we walk the Cataract Falls Trail. I'd never been on it. Thanks to Suzanne I've been on many trails since my strokes that I'd never been on before my strokes — trails I doubt I ever would have been on without the incentive to live fully that my strokes brought me.

The Cataract Falls Trail is on the backside of the moun-tain; its name captures the stunning changes that happen along the trail in the winter. No other part of the mountain has such glorious waterfalls. Although I'd heard about the trail, I had only a vague idea of what the experience would be like. Suzanne and I drove down the mountain to the trailhead at the bottom of the mountain and set off.

To experience the falls as they tumbled in roaring, laugh-ing torrents down the mountain, we had to go up very steeply. Rocks jutted out of the mountain to form steps, uneven dis-tances apart, some so high they required very strong legs. Many of the rocks were mossy and slippery. This was a chal-lenging trail, and certainly one I never would have attempted on my own. Suzanne stood beside me, allowing me to make the steps I could do on my own, and giving me a hand up or down on the steps too challenging for me. The sights and sounds and smells were every bit as beautiful as I'd heard. And I got to experience them. I climbed Cataract Falls Trail! It was a glorious day — one I'll never forget.

When Suzanne took me on that amazing hike, she did more than take me to a beautiful place. She made an experi-ence possible for me that I didn't have the ability to create by myself. She bridged me. She stood beside me. She modeled the behavior, the moves, and the patterns that I needed to move my body. She taught me to be agile and strong.

As we grow our center in strength, we're able to be more effective bridges for one another. Bringing our strength to stand beside one another and demonstrating how things can be done, we bridge one another into new possibilities. My therapists and family and friends did this for me throughout my recovery. Now I was discovering that I could take what I'd learned about transformation and do this for other people: help them by bridging them into possibility.

I healed from my strokes from the inside out. Even the muscles of my face, my ability to form words and to speak, healed from the center outward. Today if I'm very tired, at the left edge of my mouth I can feel the difficulty of moving those muscles. That's the part that healed last. Healing from the center outward taught me time and time again the power of strength from the center. Just as my strokes taught me how to walk using my trunk muscles, they taught me that if I held myself strong at the core, my ability to move through the world would change fundamentally from what it had been before. When my center was strong, everything I did took less effort.

Meditation — or whatever form of spiritual practice we engage in — is a kind of inner weight lifting for developing strength in the center of ourselves. As my heart was torn open through my strokes, I opened to the opportunity to let go of everything else and find a way to hold my inner center in strength. From the center, I could find a way to move through the world. My heart could flower again because there was a safe and strong container to hold it. When there's strength in the center, we don't effort so hard. Our stance is wider, more stable, and our strength flows more deeply.

Recovery — healing from the inside out — requires an internal move toward deep kindness and strength. We discover a new balance in the center of our being — a new way to explore and live and listen. Kindness and strength and uncompromising truth. As we're called upon to witness the terrible beauty of life, so we can help one another. If I'm facing difficulty and you're willing to stand with me, bridging me, and witnessing the difficulty with love and compassion, then I carry within me a seed — an example of how I can witness my own life with love and compassion. That seed is the beginning of possibility.

## CHAPTER TWENTY-FOUR

# *Eight Principles of Transformation*

WHEN POSSIBILITIES BEGIN TO EMERGE, we can develop our ability to work with them. We can put the lessons of transformation into practice. Simply put, the lessons I learned in the course of my recovery naturally group into eight basic principles of transformation:

> *It's the how — not the what.*
> *Show up.*
> *Open your heart.*
> *Start from where you are.*
> *Be skillful.*
> *Practice self-care.*
> *Let go.*
> *Get out of the way.*

I learned these lessons by living them. I watched these lessons unfold in my body and my life. They didn't come from an intellectual exercise that I read about somewhere. I discovered them by practice at its most raw and most powerful.

I'll never forget this profound teaching. Every move my body makes reminds me of what I learned.

Since 2005, I've shared these principles with patients in rehab, and I've watched them put the knowledge into practice to change their lives. And in the world outside of rehab, I've also seen over and over again how these principles can transform whatever difficulties people encounter. These principles continue to transform my own life. I know they work. I've seen them in action.

## IT'S THE HOW — NOT THE WHAT

When I had my strokes, I thought my world had broken apart. I was convinced that my useful life was over, that I would never do anything really productive and beneficial again. I couldn't imagine that I'd be anything or accomplish anything that would make a difference.

I've been wrong many times in my life, and doubtless I will be wrong many times more, but I've never been that wrong.

Working with my strokes has taught me, as perhaps nothing else could have, that it's truly not what happens that matters. It's not the *what*. I had two devastating strokes, strokes that by so-called objective standards — whatever those might be — indicated that my life was now officially a disaster zone. I could have collapsed around that view, and my life would have remained exactly that: a self-centered black hole into which other people's energy drained. Instead, taking what I knew from my life and spiritual practice, I did what I could with what I had. That's the *how*.

The facts of my strokes were the same either way. What

was different was how I approached these facts. How I approached the facts changed the outcome in ways I would never have dreamed possible, and profoundly changed the lives of the people who shared the journey, as well as my own. What we do with and about the situations of our lives changes everything.

How we deal with what happens is what matters. Any circumstance, any difficulty, can be transformed by the approach we bring to it. What looks like a great disaster, in fact, may offer the greatest opportunity for us to have the biggest impact we will ever have not only on our own lives but also on the lives of the people around us.

In the Jewish tradition, we're called to "make this moment holy." We make the moment holy by recognizing its wholeness. We do not really make it holy ourselves. Every moment is *already* holy — whole and complete in and of itself. There's nothing we can do that will change that truth; we aren't *that* powerful. Instead, what we're called to do is to recognize and be aware of the wholeness. In every situation, we encounter an opportunity to act in a way that communicates to those around us that we're aware of this wholeness. When we do this — when we respond to whatever happens with a willingness to work with what is, just as it is, not knowing the outcome, trusting in the unfolding — when we meet the challenges of our lives, we help the people around us see the possibility that they too can do the same. When they do, they're relieved of some of their own suffering. How we approach what happens to us opens possibilities for everyone around us.

How do we do this? In simple ways, essentially by incorporating the principles that the strokes taught me: the lessons of showing up and taking responsibility for our lives, of opening our hearts with love and kindness, of paying attention to where we are, of being skillful, of taking care of ourselves, of letting go, and of getting our egos out of the way. These practices are all we really need in order to celebrate and demonstrate the wholeness of any moment. My strokes taught me that practicing these principles when we're already relatively happy or cheerful, when these practices seem relatively easy, prepares us for when things are difficult. If we practice them in our daily lives, right now, whatever our circumstances, they will be there when we really need them.

Just because we're suffering, just because something has happened that causes us suddenly to become aware of the reality of suffering, doesn't make a moment broken or less than whole. The moment is still whole and complete in itself. Our suffering is part of it, and we can and do choose how we respond to that suffering. When the dark times come, we can collapse or we can continue our practice of recognizing the moment as whole. When we acknowledge the wholeness and meet our suffering with compassion and a willingness to work, we find we're given a means to come through our difficulties with peace in our hearts and the opportunity to change the outcome of whatever happens to us.

## SHOW UP

Showing up means being willing to take on the challenges of our own lives. It means taking responsibility for ourselves and our lives. We sometimes think of taking responsibility as an onerous task, something that nobody else wants to do and we're stuck with it — a bit like taking out the garbage. But being responsible doesn't mean we have to do something all by ourselves. Life is a team effort. Being responsible simply means we're willing to be accountable for being the creative director of the living project called "me" — that we recognize that we, not someone else, are the ones who respond to what life brings us.

My beloved Bob had a wonderful way with words. He often took them apart and gave them a greater meaning. One of his favorite words to do this to was the word *responsible*. Bob always pronounced it as *response-able*. By this, he meant that we can choose from moment to moment if we're willing and able to respond to what life gives us. To take responsibility for what we do with what happens to us is fundamentally a choice. It's a choice whether we think it is or not. If we don't show up and take responsibility, we're still making a choice — the choice of not being *response-able*.

Sometimes I'd say to Bob, "I can't do this." He would look me in the eye and say, "Won't, not can't." He frequently reminded me that as long as I'm alive I have the power of choice in every circumstance I encounter. Saying "can't" meant giving up responsibility before I started. Saying "won't" acknowledged my power to change.

Until we're willing to show up and be *response-able*, we are, in some sense, victims of what happens to us. What's the point of that? If the choice is either being passive and giving up when something difficult comes my way or showing up

and doing my best with it, I'd much rather see what I can do.
If nothing else, it's a lot more interesting. And as I've learned,
I just might discover that I can do more than I ever dreamed.

When we decide to show up, we take responsibility. We
know that we're the architects of our own lives, we face forward, and we give ourselves the opportunity to build what
we believe in.

## OPEN YOUR HEART

Opening the heart is fierce work. In our world, all too often
we think that if we open our hearts, we'll somehow become
mushy and weak and lose our determination, but this is an
inaccurate view of what it means to open the heart. Opening
the heart requires strength and courage and the willingness
to be powerful. Compassion and love are the most powerful forces for change that I've ever witnessed. Consider
Mahatma Gandhi. Consider Martin Luther King Jr. Those
men believed in opening the heart, and they changed the
world.

When I open my heart, I let myself be touched directly
by the life around me. But when I close my heart, I cut myself
off. If I'm injured, or if I have a problem of any kind, I need
all the ability to work with and deal with what is in front of me
that I can find. I want to be as much in touch with life, and as
nourished by it, as I can be. Life reaches out to me if I'm willing to let it.

When I walk toward my house from the garage in the
early evening, with darkness settling on the trees like a cloak,

the owls *hoo-hoo* to one another across my path, touching me with wonder. If I closed my heart, I would never really hear them. With an open heart, my sense of wonder gives me fresh eyes. As a child is able to look at the world without judgment, when I open my heart and experience a sense of wonder, I see more. I don't close myself to possibility.

On a very fundamental level, closing my heart closes *all* of me. All our parts work together. If I want to be teachable — to open my mind and truly be willing to learn what I can do to help myself — I must open my heart. Love and compassion, kindness and hope, fill the spaces in an open heart. They increase my strength to face what must be faced, to see what can be seen, and to learn what I need to know.

When we open our hearts, we cultivate a positive attitude. We remember to laugh and love, to live our lives now — with no waiting.

## START FROM WHERE YOU ARE

Think of an iceberg. Most of an iceberg isn't visible. If we look at an iceberg from the water surface, we see only a small part of the whole. Our lives and our challenges are often like icebergs. Much of what's really happening takes place beneath the surface, where we don't see and don't choose to look. In order to work with our lives and our challenges, we need to learn to look.

Before my strokes, I thought I knew a fair amount about my life, but what I mostly knew were stories I made up about what might be below the surface of what I was actually paying attention to. I wasn't really looking. When I'd start a project, I'd be in a big hurry to get to the end of it. "Immediately make it something different and move on" was my motto. None of that helped me start from where I was.

Now I say, "What is, is." I don't have to tell myself a story about it. I don't have to immediately make it go away by changing it. The more I'm willing to look at what is, just as it is, the more information I have. The more information I have, the more I'm able to take wise action when the time is right.

Growing up, we generally receive little training in this skill. Our lives are so often competitive that we're encouraged to look good rather than speak the truth. The standard greeting when somebody asks us how we are is "Fine." We're taught not to look too closely at how we truly are. And if, by chance, we do have a pretty fair idea of how our lives are going, we're taught to pretend things are different from our actual experience of them; we're taught to tell a story about them. When we pretend long enough, we stop looking — and no longer can even tell ourselves the truth.

The less we like or approve of something, the less attention we're likely to pay to it. But paying close attention to what we don't like is critical if we want to change things. Paying attention to what is, just as it is, without pretending or prejudging, allows us to start from where we are. Because we've so often ignored much of what we could know, we need to learn to pay attention by practicing. We train ourselves, and when we do, with our hearts open, we give ourselves the ability to look and to know.

How often have I seen people try to start from where they imagine themselves to be or where they wish they were. So much energy is wasted that way. Starting from where we are makes all the energy we expend more useful and more efficient. We don't waste whatever resources we have. We take action in a focused, effective way. When we know where our feet are, all the steps we take are purposeful.

Starting from where we are, we pay attention. We create goals we can achieve one after another, we break old habits, and we challenge our preconceived notions of what's possible.

## BE SKILLFUL

Magical thinking tells us that if we just think good thoughts and are nice people, everything will work out just fine. No work required. That's not my experience. My experience is that thinking good thoughts is very important, but it won't get me where I want to go by itself. The more I'm willing to work and learn to work smarter, the better my chances for positive change will be. That's being skillful.

If I want a clean dish, I can't leave the baked-on-cheese-covered plate sitting on the counter and wish it to be clean. Where I live, all I would get is some flies coming in to walk around on the dish. If I want to accomplish something, I need to show up and do my best with it and keep on learning how to do it better. I need to make the effort to wash the dish as well as I can today. Tomorrow I might be able to do it better, but what I have to work with is today. I don't worry about whether or not I could do it better tomorrow. I do the best I can today.

Being skillful also entails knowing what I can and what I can't do and getting help with what I need help with. If I want to clean that dish and need soap, but I can't drive to the store to get it, being skillful is asking someone to do the shopping for me. Then I have the soap and can manage the part of the task that I can do.

It's a mistake to think that if we aren't a concert violinist we can't pick up the violin, or if we're not a world-class athlete we can't throw a ball. We can all be skillful in the ways we are, right now. Building our lives means using ourselves and the abilities and strengths we currently possess as wisely as we can at any moment, learning as we go and asking for help when we need it. It isn't about some idea of having to be "perfect" before we even start.

When we're skillful, we know that we can make a difference. We don't give up, and we work with what we have, growing our abilities as we move through our lives.

## PRACTICE SELF-CARE

This week as I've been working on this book, I've given myself the gift of regular exercise. Right now I'd love to spend the next several hours glued to this computer, but instead I'm going to go ride an exercise bike. I'm tempted to wear myself out writing, but I won't. Why not? Because if I do, what I write won't be as graceful or as honest as it will be if I take a break and go ride that bike. My body needs the exercise. When I give it exercise, I feel better, I sleep better, and I think better. I also smile more. That's one aspect of self-care in action.

We want to build our lives, and our lives are the expressions of who we are. If we make ourselves miserable by abusing ourselves, what kind of life can we build? We sabotage ourselves from the start when we don't take care of the very place from which the satisfaction and joy in life arise: ourselves. Other people aren't going to distill their joy and sense of a life well lived and turn it into a pill for us to swallow. We have only one instrument available to us to use to build our lives. That's this body, this mind, and this spirit — what we've been issued for this life. Taking care of ourselves makes sense.

Self-care is grounded in forgiveness. When we judge ourselves harshly without forgiveness for our mistakes, we tend to treat ourselves badly, to punish ourselves. When we judge another harshly for their mistakes, we harden our hearts, which is another form of self-punishment. Forgiveness allows us to hold ourselves with the tenderness and mercy that self-care requires. Remember Bob's admonition that "to love another person, we must first love ourselves"? When we truly love ourselves and others, we find in our hearts the means to forgive.

It took me a long time to learn this lesson. More than fifty years. It also took having so few abilities poststroke that taking care of what I had became an obvious choice. We don't have to wait until we're desperate to practice self-care. When we take care of ourselves every moment, we give ourselves so many more opportunities for rich lives. If I could, I would teach self-care in elementary school to every kid I could find.

Realizing how much of my own life I made miserable by the way I treated myself is a humbling lesson.

When we practice self-care, we take care of ourselves, we minimize the stresses in our lives, and we're intentionally kind to ourselves. We deal lovingly and wisely with ourselves and the people who love us.

## LET GO

At one point in my life I was determined to control what was happening in my life. Where I got the idea that such a thing was possible, I'll never know. A life can be influenced, shaped, or directed. It can be opened up or embellished with love and laughter. But one thing it can't be is controlled. Life is uncertain, abundant with circumstances outside our ability to predict, much less control. Fundamentally that's a good thing, because it means that life is filled with possibility.

The infinite nature of possibility is inherently unimaginable. What we can imagine is only a tiny portion of what's truly possible. There's so much truth to the old cliché "Truth is stranger than fiction." By stubbornly believing that we're in charge and in control, that we can imagine all that's possible, we can and often do narrow our view, refusing to see what might really be possible.

So many times during my recovery, I learned the value of the lesson of having no story, the lesson that my friend Betty Joan taught me the day she said, "Nobody knows." So many times during my recovery I worked not knowing what outcome might come from my efforts. Every time I was willing to do this, every time I stayed in the present moment and didn't try to control what was happening, what *actually* happened was beyond my ability to imagine. By being willing to let go and not try to control or to predict, but instead trusting that possibilities will appear, we remove the blinders from our eyes. We begin to see and appreciate what's present. When we do this, we give ourselves the opportunity to work with the limitless, unfolding possibilities all around us.

## GET OUT OF THE WAY

Before my strokes, I was standing in the way of my own life. This sounds like a paradox, a contradiction in terms, but it was all too true. I'd accomplished a reasonable number of external goals, which looked good, like decorations on a Christmas tree, but every achievement was a struggle arising from my self-preoccupation. Was I good enough? Did I do enough? Was I smart enough? Strong enough? Agile enough? Thorough enough? Attractive enough? What were the people next to me doing? Were they better at whatever it was than I was? Was the life I imagined that they led so much better than mine? I traveled a lot on business. I would sit in airports and compare myself to people I'd never met, whose lives I had no way of knowing, and I'd feel envious of lives that were fabrications of my own imagination.

Or I would try to make myself feel useful by "helping" someone else when what I was really doing was trying to fix them, trying to decide for them what and who they should be, which is another form of comparison. This kind of comparison is envy flipped onto its other side: conceit.

Comparison and envy constrict the heart in ways beyond

our easy understanding. When I compare myself to others and envy them and think, "If only," I close down my capacity to love and accept who I am in this present moment.

And when I think, "Oh, I need to help these people because they need to be fixed in some way, and I can help to fix them," I'm equally closing down my heart and ceasing to be who I can be in this present moment.

My strokes humbled me; they taught me that it was more than okay to be what I am — an ordinary person, like any other, working with what I have. I don't need to be a this label or a that label — a manager, a businessperson, an artist, a housewife — or any label at all. I'm just a person faced with the pieces of my own life.

I'm no more, and no less, important or valuable or competent than any other human being. Knowing and accepting this is a gift beyond measure. It allows me to simply be where I am — no closing of the heart, no comparison, no "If onlys," no wishing to be what I'm not. The truth of who I am is all I have to bring to any situation. The moment I wish to be what I'm not, I can't be just here, just now. I can't live the creative expression of my own heart. When I live the truth of who I am — a human being like any other with all my individual quirks — the possibilities that open are endless.

The eight principles of transformation I outlined in this chapter can help with any challenge. Again, they are:

*It's the how — not the what.*

*Show up.*

*Open your heart.*

*Start from where you are.*

*Be skillful.*

*Practice self-care.*

*Let go.*

*Get out of the way.*

Using these eight principles has enriched my life in more ways than I could have believed possible. I invite you to try them and see if they make a difference in your life.

# Afterword

BEFORE MY STROKES I thought I understood generosity, but I didn't. I thought if I had five apples and I gave you one, I was generous. If I gave you two, I was even more generous. And if I gave you three or four, only keeping one or two for myself, I was really, really generous. I thought of generosity as a zero-sum game. There was only so much to go around, and what was given to one person was lost to another.

Now I know that even though I was often thought of as a generous person, I really didn't have a clue what true generosity was. When I began to open my heart to working with other people to share what I'd learned from my strokes — when I put what I knew into service to help others — the front door of my heart opened. But when I wasn't looking, the back door of my heart opened too. And then the windows opened, and the side doors, and the skylights. Soon, what I was giving out the front door wasn't even close to what was pouring into my life through all the other openings.

As my heart kept opening in generosity, I couldn't begin to give away the blessings that were pouring into my heart and into my life. And then I understood that it wasn't about *me* at all. One more time, all I needed to do was use what I'd learned and get out of the way. This experience of true generosity is the most life-giving experience I know. It took two strokes to teach me this. If you had told me seven years ago when I lay in that hospital bed that someday I would feel grateful for this lesson, I would have thought you were mad. Nothing good seemed like it could come from what had happened to me. Nothing could be worth such a cost, I thought. Today I have no doubt it was a price worth paying.

My experience throughout my recovery is that life unfolds in ways we can't predict. If you encounter a difficult challenge in your own life, I hope you'll remember that this challenge doesn't have to define or limit you. You hold an amazing power to influence the course of your own life. How you respond to the challenges of your life can become your opportunity to discover just how much you have to give to yourself, this world, and the people in it. May you find possibility and the blessings of generosity in whatever you encounter.

# Acknowledgments

T HERE ARE SO MANY PEOPLE TO THANK for the wonders of my life these days. I name only some of them. All the rest — all the other people who touch my life — please know that if I haven't named you here, it's solely for the purpose of some brevity. I hold you all with great gratitude.

My family: First and foremost, my beloved husband, Bob — though he is no longer an embodied presence on this world, his memory is a constant source of strength and purpose; my sons, Fletcher and Jacob, those tenderhearted men who held and hold me in their love and strength; my brother, Jeff, whose choice to live beside me sustains me in ways he'll never know; my father and mother, John and Dorothy, also now gone, from whom I learned to face the world; my stepmother, Evelyn, who has become my friend; and Gene and Karen, who took care of Bob when I could not.

All the people at the Kaiser Permanente hospitals and the Kaiser Foundation Rehabilitation Center, whose dedication and care change so many lives — most especially all those I mention in this book, without whom I would not be writing anything.

My friends: Stanley, who taught me how to show up in my own life; Bonnie, who has become like a daughter to me; Martha, now gone, who healed my heart; Suzanne, whose inventive and joyful approach to life inspires us all; Rita, whose courage never fails to blow me away; Carol, who gives so much and holds it all with such integrity; Betty Joan, companion and doctor extraordinaire, who stood beside me day after day; Ilana, who gave her laughter and expertise with so much care; Sara, who cheered me on; Paul, my coproducer, and his lovely wife, Barbara, who challenged me to know that I could make a difference; and Jan and Roy, who helped me see that consulting and transformation have the same source.

All my neighbors, especially Marge, Andy, Phil, Del, Steve, Barney, Etta, and Arthur.

John and all the members of the Thursday meditation group, who have become my *sangha*, my spiritual community.

Nathan, who made a mystical bridge to Judaism that I could cross.

The board, faculty, administration, and students of Saybrook, who called me back to an active life after Bob died.

And my dear friend and publisher Linda Kramer, who believed in me when I had no hope and who makes this book and so many other life-changing books possible.

# About the Author

ALISON BONDS SHAPIRO works with stroke survivors and their families, provides motivational speaking for rehabilitation patients and their care networks in numerous locations including a leading HMO in Northern California, and is an advisor to a nonprofit dedicated to stroke survivors. She is also a highly regarded business consultant and transformational coach and leads the board of trustees of a graduate school in San Francisco. Alison lives, works, and paints in her home in the woods on Mt. Tamalpais outside of San Francisco, which she shares with her brother, Jeff, her cat, Sam, and the love and laughter of the frequent visits of her sons and grandsons.

For more information, please visit
www.healingintopossibility.com.

H J Kramer and New World Library are dedicated to
publishing books and audio products that inspire
and challenge us to improve the quality
of our lives and our world.

Our products are available
in bookstores everywhere.
For our catalog, please contact:

H J Kramer / New World Library
14 Pamaron Way
Novato, California 94949

Phone: (415) 884-2100 or (800) 972-6657
Catalog requests: Ext. 50
Orders: Ext. 52
Fax: (415) 884-2199

E-mail: escort@newworldlibrary.com
Website: www.newworldlibrary.com